REDUCED TO A WHISPER

DEBBIE WADE

ABOVE THE SUN

The Coaching Connection

TCCDecide.com

Published by Above The Sun

AboveTheSun.org

Printed in the United States of America

Paperback ISBN: 978-1-952385-21-6

Hardback ISBN: 978-1-952385-22-3

eBook ISBN: 978-1-952385-20-9

CONTENTS

Mom, you missed the opportunity to write the book that was in your heart. But you inspired me to write and you loved me well. There is never a day that passes that I don't miss you. I honor you and thank God for the gift that you were in our lives. It was your gentle nudge that gave me the courage to face my fear and publish this, so I dedicate this one to you.

INTRODUCTION

What started as a journal has evolved over two decades into this book. This is my living tapestry, depicting scenes from an ordinary woman's life, one who was desperately seeking Truth and her true identity. Alone, I would have been left only knowing the knotted, tangled mass of the seemingly insignificant threads of my existence. But I discovered that I could hear the voice of God and feel His Presence, and His words of encouragement would continually unveil the finished side of this tapestry.

Over the years, I have experienced the same truth as the prophet, Elijah. *The Lord was not in the wind that was so strong that it was splitting mountains and breaking rocks in pieces. He was not in the earthquake or fire.* 1 Kings 19:11-12, NRSV) I was being trained to recognize the Whisper of His voice heard within sheer silence.

He has not changed. He still speaks, *Let there be light.* And there it is—revelation... understanding... His perspective... bringing peace. His ways, His interpretation of my circumstances helps my mind to bend, my thoughts to shift, my heart to soften, my emotions to settle, and there is rest. This process takes time, listening time, alert and hushed... moments that I have to fight for.

My son wrote a song a few years back that I believe captures the spirit of the age. There is a line in the chorus that says, "Everybody talking but nobody listens, nobody listen, nobody listen." (Nobody Listen, Lifehouse)

Never in the history of mankind have we ever been so inundated with noise and distraction. We now have at our fingertips devices that have the potential to fill our ears, eyes and minds with everything imaginable. The cell phone, iPad and computer have captured the attention of all, from infants to the elderly. They offer an endless variety of options, from movies and games to minute by minute updates on absolutely everything and everybody.

For many, these devices are consuming every waking hour of the day with ongoing clatter. It's not that I don't appreciate the benefits of this technological age. I just wonder—what will be the ongoing fruit of the new habits being established, in some cases, addictions that are actually being embraced? What is happening to our ability to think critically and have common sense? What is behind the growing disconnect between our ability to know the difference between right and wrong? What happened to our ability to love and accept others who have differing opinions, not to mention authentic relational connection? What happened to the value of rest and peace and quiet reflection? And what has become of the skill of listening, not only to others but especially to our Creator?

I have spent a lifetime learning the value of stepping back, stopping the onslaught of busyness, saying no to distractions and bridling my thoughts into submission. I have been on a mission to train myself to be aware of the hidden spiritual realities, to dig for the treasured nuggets that are unseen and to listen for Wisdom's voice, which is available to all but can only be heard within the environment of solitude. This journey has led me to the True

Source of all that is good and right. I have discovered Life which is embodied within a deep relationship with the Godhead.

If you are a seeker, if you are worn out from the hectic, empty existence that we have created, and if you are longing for a fulfilling, joyful pathway to lead you into a restful Presence, then this book is for you. When someone is whispering and you want to hear them, you must lean in to hear them. To think deeply, you need quiet. You need time. You must draw away. *Reduced to a Whisper* is an invitation into a spiritual, relational connection with our Divine Family, which happens naturally as we disconnect from the things of this world. If we reduce the noise, reduce the busyness, if we choose to reduce the clutter of fruitless activity, we eventually find ourselves returning to our roots—walking and talking with our Creator in a garden of simplicity, drinking deeply from the Living Water that flows within us. And because we are in the Presence of Awe, we find that we are the ones who are reduced to a whisper.

Leaning In

Each time we come face to face with a new awareness of Truth, we are at a crossroads. I felt strongly that our Holy Counselor had opened a window of opportunity for unusual breakthroughs. His words to me were, *"If we lean in to hear His voice and make a choice to change our thinking, exponential growth is possible."* As a life coach, I want to maximize your opportunity for growth and offer some powerful questions at the end of each chapter which might assist you in this process. My prayer is that as you hear my stories, you might *lean in* and find God within yours.

Stand at the crossing, and consider the ancient path, for it is good and it leads to Me. Walk on this path, and you will find rest for your souls. (Jeremiah 6:16, The Voice)

1

FALL

THE RELEASE OF AN IDENTITY

For the past few years, I have been on a quest, a journey of discovery. It began in November as I knelt beside my mother's bed. Her breathing changed in the wee hours of the morning. There was a warm Holy Presence of Peace, allowing our hearts to embrace for one last long hug. Each breath was followed by an increasing stillness. I could feel her reluctance to leave and yet in the deep hush, I felt an unexpected excitement for her, knowing that she was finally standing at the doorway of her heart's desire—to be with Jesus. I will always treasure this moment. This was our last mother-daughter experience together on this side of eternity. It is sacred to me. It was my mother's arms that held me when the Breath of God first entered my newborn lungs. Now, as her daughter, I was given the honor of holding her as she was released into the whisper of His voice calling her home.

I don't understand how it happened, but that same gentle call began a release within my own heart that day. Perhaps it was Mom's last prayer for me as she caught a glimpse of her own heavenly identity.

I awoke this morning aching for her. Maybe because summer

is coming to an end and November is quickly approaching. The frosty morning air nips at my toes. With the chill, every shade of yellow, orange, gold and red have been splattered throughout the countryside. It is as if the Master Gardener has splashed His warmth through the full spectrum of autumn hues, transforming our landscape. My hand steadies the hot mug of coffee as a chill moves down my spine. I can feel them both—Mom and our Comforter.

A smile lifts my cheek as I peer out at the hills behind my home. They are covered with evergreens—pine trees, spruce, firs and my favorite, the cedar. She assumes her majestic stance and rises tall amongst them all. Each one appears to be so confident and steady, able to bend and sway in a heavenly dance that awakens my heart to the possibilities of a fulfilled life.

I am mesmerized by the view stretching across our nine acres. As I behold the boundless diversity of color and texture, I am awestruck by the nobility that stands before me. The gentle breeze and the song of the birds create a stillness in my mind, enabling me to hear their story, and I am moved by their tune.

It has been a fruitful year. Our apple trees have produced a bountiful crop, and they have served us well. Now with the coming of winter, they willingly yield to the gentle breeze of their Creator the very leaves that once covered and defined them. They will stand shamelessly bare in the days to come and very still as we prune them, embracing the wisdom that the loving cut from our gardener will surely bring increase for the coming year.

I found myself wanting to stand and applaud them, but the ache within my chest would not allow me to move. Oh, that I would be so in tune with my Maker, so assured of His tender touch that I would gladly release the stronghold—MY will, MY control, over MY life!

As if in response to my thoughts, there began a crescendo in the sound of the wind stirring the trees. The lyrics being sung were not just stroking all of my senses, but somehow they were opening a window within my soul to embrace the words of my mysterious, soothing Comforter.

"That's what Love does. That is what Jesus did for you. gladly released... control... His life... for yours."

I have tasted of God's goodness, and the wonder of His kindness in sending His Son leaves me with a longing that cries, I want to change. Father, who do YOU say that I am? Like these trees, He has planted me. His forgiveness has been the root system that has nourished and sustained me. And in His mercy, the autumn winds continue to strip me.

Come Away with Me

My thoughts returned to Mom as I relived our last moments together. Following her death, my two children both left home to follow their own dreams. I awoke one morning and realized that this was the first time in my entire life that I had ever lived totally alone. I had learned to be a survivor. For five years following my divorce, every waking hour I was consumed with the weight of responsibility to provide and care for my children. Now, as I found myself peering into the "empty nest", a gentle nudge, "*Come away with Me*", began to draw my weary soul into a place of rest that I had never known before. The more time I spent in the quiet solitude with Jesus, the more I craved it.

The stress of survival living had wound me up so tight that it took a full two years to retrain my mind to be still and my body to relax. Many times, I felt like an overactive two-year-old. It seemed impossible to sit and just be quiet. My mind would continually wander off, and then I would run back to His side just to make sure He was still there.

Those were the days of an awakening, a dawning that revealed the hidden places in my heart. I began to realize what a performer

I had become. The motive behind almost everything I did was to please. As a child, I wanted the approval of Mom and Dad, so I made a valiant attempt to be the perfect daughter. I was driven to be quiet, obedient and helpful.

As a young girl, I gave up playing "house" and "dolls", and instead I dug out the underbrush and helped to create forts with my brothers. I climbed trees and constructed tree houses. If I was to be accepted by my three brothers, I had to fit into their world, so I pushed myself (unsuccessfully, I might add) to out-run, out-climb and even out-fight them. The interesting thing is that even though outwardly I had become a pretty accomplished tom-boy, my true girly side would continually manifest. Our forts were the cleanest, the most organized hangouts in the county.

I carried the same pleasing drive right into my marriage. I would do anything, be whatever he wanted me to be. Being a performer and perfectionist brings a whole lot of pressure into a marriage. There was an empty, cold cavern of loneliness in my heart for as long as I could remember. The feelings of isolation increased, even if I was in the presence of those whom I loved.

I don't think I had ever really felt accepted, appreciated or really known by anyone. But how could I? I was lost even to myself. My heart was longing for something or someone tangible who would fill the emptiness and "make me happy." I was seeking approval and validation, but I was listening to the wrong voices. I had enthroned people in my heart, looking to man to define me rather than my Creator. I had unknowingly given my permission and power to man to fashion me into an image that lacked my authentic design. Instead of inviting Him to fill my deepest desires for love and significance, the burden was placed on those closest to me. The results were excruciating.

In the moments of quiet reflection, I began to experience the accepting heart of Jesus. It was my choice to turn off the noise around me, and I could sense His pleasure with that decision.

After work, I'd lace up my tennis shoes and head for the hills. I craved this—to just walk and think and pray. No phone, no music —just the peaceful sounds of nature mixed with a bit of static from traffic in the distance, which was always a reminder of the pace of life from which I was desperately trying to escape.

Some days I was too exhausted to walk, so I would allow myself to fall onto the couch and soak in the heavy, peaceful solitude and just breathe His name. There were times that I would jump in the car, imagine that He was in the passenger seat and we would drive for miles into the countryside. We shared walks on the beach, watching the sunset, stargazing—so many joyful moments, and many without any words being spoken at all.

Over the years, this decision to be still has increasingly become a lifestyle. I'm not sure why I crave silence. Maybe it is just because I am an introvert. Or maybe it is that I am desperately in love and in need of Him, this Mysterious, Unseen Partner who brings me true Life. It is here, in this atmosphere of stillness, that I am more apt to find Him and able to hear His voice. Most often, I don't feel His presence at all, but I have been trained to just KNOW that whether I feel anything or not, He is always there. I asked Jesus once why faith was so important to Him. The thought that went through my mind was, "*Because when you choose to believe and put your faith in Me, it ushers you into My world. I have so much that I want to share with you. Someday this will be your home.*"

I listened as He spoke, silencing the echo of my past. He spoke of freedom and life. I would read His words in the Gospels and personalize them. I would imagine myself in the stories, imagine His face, ask Him questions and then listen for His answers in my thoughts. His encouragement and laughter was like rain softening the soil of my heart. He gave me the courage to dig below the surface of my actions and revealed that my deepest motives were most often unhealthy and diseased.

Much of the fruit that I produced in my life was severely dwarfed by the mutated cells of performance, guilt, insecurity and fear. This discovery process was not complicated. But it was one that required courage and honesty and a faith expectancy to hear both Him and my own heart speak. My Holy Coach would ask a simple question like, "*What do you think made you react that way?*" or "*What were you trying to achieve through that action?*" or "*What is it that you need that you're not getting in that relationship?*"

These types of questions led me into a place of deep introspection. But because I was not alone, because He was always there with me, I could face the fear of the lurking unknown. I could hear the lies that my heart was believing. I was an incredible mess seen through my eyes. But not through His. He was always calm and so kind. My honest admission of guilt was always met with a smile of acceptance and many times with a humorous grin and question like, "*How's that working out for you?*" Sometimes my insane logic just made us both laugh to the point of tears. What a relief! To be seen, to be known, to not be shamed, just accepted.

At times I was experiencing rebirth. At times it was dark and I could feel parts of me dying. There were seasons of clearing and planting and growing... and times of harvest. I identify with these fruit trees. What once covered and defined me in the previous seasons of my existence are gradually being blown away by Holy Breath. I, too, stand exposed before Him in humble vulnerability, releasing the old and expectantly awaiting the new.

To me, the earthly seasons are but the guardians of time as I know it. I appreciate a sense of stability or an appointed order around which our small lives revolve. But in reality, they simply serve and obey the One who spoke this world into existence. I am finding that when we slow down, it is possible to sense a rhythm—or is it a heartbeat? It woos us to live and move and have our being in sync with Another.

. . .

The Invitation

This invitation to come away with Him, to give up control and bask in His perfect peace is for every one of His children, not just me. He is no respecter of persons. His desire is for all to share life with Him, for all to enter His domain, to explore the depth, the height, the breadth and width of true LOVE. It is only here that our chaotic existence on this planet has any hope of finding authentic resolve. This is where we can discover Jesus, the Author of Life. As we do, we find ourselves relaxing more and more into the comfort and contentment of just getting to be our true selves, imperfect for sure, but basking in the assurance of being completely loved and unconditionally accepted by the Divine.

Who I am is not so much determined by what I do anymore, or what everyone thinks about me and certainly NOT by the mistakes I have made and will continue to make. All that really matters, in the end, is WHOSE I am! Where does my allegiance lie? Who am I living for? This growing faith Relationship is the created, sacred priority which has ultimately refined my choices and continues to shape my being. The deepening tap root of surrendered love and pleasure within our Connection grounds me.

Sadly, it has only been recently that I have discovered a whole new depth, an experiential dimension of Grace and Mercy that undergirds my motivation to invest in this mysterious flow of Oneness that exists in the unseen realm of my being. Yes, I have faith in Him, but He has faith in me, even when I don't believe in myself. He is content with me. In the midst of all my flaws and immaturity, Grace consistently models how to approach myself with gentleness and kindness. Holy Comfort relentlessly seeks me out when I seem to be driven to all the false comforts that are available in this world.

This is a very different God than the one who was introduced to me as a child in church. This Master is not like the life-long religious taskmaster occupying my mind who has beaten me down and forced me to strive for perfection. He is not demanding and harsh. He enjoys me, and His attitude is contagious. Each and every new dawn offers an enticement of fresh Mercy, and I awaken hearing His voice beckoning me to come, to choose Him, the Life-giver. We share in the excitement of exploring the freedom that is available as we approach each new day as if it were the first.

This raw awareness of how He feels about us is where change becomes possible. It is becoming my new reality, a place where stillness and the warmth of acceptance permeate the atmosphere and I can grow. There is no judgment or comparison here, so it is not so scary to try new things. The word "failure" loses its power and is replaced with a passion for learning. This is where we can learn to walk in the confidence that we are dearly loved children. Here, patience gives space to think creatively. We are not rushed or pushed or crowded. We are just invited in, encouraged to discover at our own pace and be true to who we were created to be and journey together on this earth and beyond. And it is available for us all.

The beauty of God's provision is that He knows if you lack an experiential grid for comprehending and entering into this heavenly reality. He knows you. He knows if you were robbed of having a loving environment in your earthly home. He knows the damage that has been done. And because He is the Creator, He is Love and He is the Healer, He is willing and able to recreate within you that which was missing or destroyed. It is yours. Just ask for it!

Staying in the Shadow of Love is where our fears can fade away. Love casts out fear. Staying is always our choice. It is deciding to be in a relationship with Him, to direct our WILL to turn in His direction, to surrender and embrace the mystery of this unseen Relationship. For me, I have decided to make Him my stronghold instead of my unbelief. Believing in what He has said and what He has promised is a decision that we get to make.

Our Creator is the Perfect Relator, and we were designed to enjoy the intimate company of Someone who cares and wants to speak life and peace into our sometimes messy, confusing lives. The moment we were born, Love breathed His Life Breath into our lungs, and as long as we are on this earth, the gift of His Passion for us enables us to love Him back. It is there, in that Union, where we receive the flow of Living Water needed to soften the soil of our hearts, enabling us to love both ourselves and others as well.

It is critical to take the time to stop and reflect and ask ourselves the difficult questions. And more importantly, to listen—to anticipate that Jesus, who is the Word, has given us everything we need to hear His voice. Enjoy the discovery process. Be still—ask, hear and think deeply, and then yield to the Pruner. See for yourself the incredible harvest that will be produced as you walk into your true identity.

It takes courage to show up in life, vulnerable and exposed and real. Courage that can only be given if we yield and follow. This could be your time. "*Come away with me*" is the invitation. To ignore it is to forfeit the ultimate gift, the very reason we exist—to be with Him, to be like Him! The true meaning of life can only be discovered within His world which we access by faith.

Reflect again on His words: "*When you choose to believe and put your faith in Me, it ushers you into My world. I have so much that I want to share with you. Someday this will be your home.*"

Leaning In:

- Who is in charge of your life?
- What in your history has come to define you?

- What areas in your life are you afraid to release to the Father? What are you believing that is causing the fear?
- In your current circumstances, what is being revealed about who you are?
- How does your Creator speak to you? What, if anything, is keeping you from hearing His voice?

God has made everything beautiful for its own time. He has planted eternity in the human heart, but even so, people cannot see the whole scope of God's work from beginning to end.
(Ecclesiastes 3:11, NLT)

2

WILDFLOWERS

OUR HIDDEN IDENTITY

Dad and I were in San Simeon, California on a cliff overlooking the ocean. There were no words being spoken. We were both enjoying the serenity of silence. Just being together was the comfort that we both needed. It is hard to describe the depth of emptiness, the immense loss I felt when Mom passed. My mother was a beautiful gift, a friend to so many, including me. She wasn't one of those energetic, charismatic leader types. She was gentle and nurturing. It was her faith in Jesus and her consistent unconditional love that left a lasting impression on my heart and continually inspired and encouraged me. Her life was not her own. It was poured out every day as she cared for her family and friends.

What would our lives be like without her? Why is it that we often fail to appreciate the gift of love that is right before us? How can we be so blind and not value and honor those who quietly serve us, until they are gone?

The rhythmic drum of the pounding waves and the blanket of warmth from the sun's rays settled my thoughts and began to ease the ache in my heart. As my body relaxed, I noticed a shift in my focus. I found myself captivated by the sight of a single, minute wildflower growing straight out of a rock. It was stunning, so dainty and somewhat concealed unless you were in no hurry and willing to linger and gaze into the hidden places. It was perfect in form, pale lavender and had a dainty, wispy elegance, and yet, it was strong enough to not only forge its existence out of the cleft of this rock but by some miracle of nature this small wonder was thriving! The surrounding landscape was rocky, and any vegetation that did exist was either dead or dying from the beatings of the wind and the blistering heat of the sun.

The backdrop of this scene became the canvas on which the Creator began to paint. Each spoken word was another brush of color bringing revelation and understanding.

"Do you know how many millions upon millions of these wildflowers I have planted in your world that no eye has ever seen? Each one is unique. They were created just for Me, for My glory."

"Wow! I have never thought about that? I wish I could be with You and see them all. This little one sure has my attention," I answered.

"I have many children like these. Hidden within the crevasses of rocky circumstances are the world's most precious, beautiful people. Like this wildflower, they could possibly go through this life without ever being noticed or having the appreciation of an observant eye. Throughout the earth in the most remote pockets of life, these are My wildflowers. Their very existence brings beauty, color, unique texture and shape to My world. They too were created for My glory, for My eye to behold."

I sighed. "Oh, Father, I love the way you think. It is so different from this world. Tell me more about these special ones."

He responded, *"These are the hidden ones, the faithful ones, the willing ones. They are content to just be, content to grow where I plant them and bloom in the most awkward, difficult of landscapes. These were not created for a cultivated garden. They do not crave the tender care of a gardener. They are hardy and determined, and the more rugged their surroundings, the more glorious they appear. So unique, so rare, so worthy!"*

Thrivers

I thought about Mom and so many other "wildflower" people that I have known. They all have one thing in common. They are more than survivors. They are thrivers! If that is not a word, it ought to be! Every day they choose life, not self-pity. These rare individuals live to serve others, not themselves. The true meaning of love is on display as each sacrificial choice frame a portrait of a loved one whose life is continually touched by heaven. I am one of those blessed ones.

As I wrote this, my mind was filled with memories, moments shared with this shy, unassuming soul. Cradled within every cell of my being, she was there. Priceless images of her compassionate smile released a fresh burst of timeless affection. I held each memory as if it were a newborn wrapped in a soft receiving blanket. Drawing them closer, I heard her singing. Even now, in her absence, she was seeking to comfort and calm my breaking heart.

For just a second, the lullaby that would mesmerize me as a child, the same lullaby that would captivate my babies and hush their crying, wondrously began its soothing magic. One breath and somehow all of my yesterdays rushed into the now and I felt her gently rocking me.

I opened my eyes to search again for the wildflower. My gaze settled on the rock and then back to the swaying slender beauty. I pondered, how is it possible? To be so frail and yet so tenacious? What secret source of life feeds your roots? What strengthens you to withstand the onslaught of the natural elements that appear determined to crush you?

A mist began to blur the image of the flower. A wave crashed in the distance, and as if on cue, I surrendered to the grief. I hid my face and listened to the sound of the rumbling water pushing its way onto the shore. The power of loss overcame me, and questions rushed at my mind like the foamy waves breaking onto the beach below. The gravity of each one was gripping. I was being pulled into the deep, one question tumbling over the next like the grains of sand being forced to retreat back into the depths of the sea.

I had very few regrets when it came to my mother until now. Wiping the salty tears off my cheek I stared at the lavender bloom. "Oh, God! Did I not see her? Did I not appreciate the gift of her relentless care? In my childishness and selfishness, did I ever attempt to enter her world? Did I really know her? What was her favorite color? Did I not take the time to notice her? To listen to her?"

I remember my mother's words to me when she found out that she had cancer. Even then she tried to cover me by saying, "Don't worry about me, honey. I am just having a temporary set-back." I watched her small fragile bones begin to break. But the disease did not crush her spirit, nor did she allow it to steal her joy. My mother lived her last days with her Lord breathing grace into her every breath. She knew where she was going. Her roots were deeply planted within the Rock of her faith. Her life was in perpetual bloom even as cancer battered and broke her body. She had practiced for decades the art of trusting in the goodness of God to always restore and redeem. His life within her produced the stamina and courage to face death with peaceful confidence. I know because I was with her when she filled her lungs for the last time.

With one more gaze, I lifted my head as the ocean breeze stroked my cheeks and caused the dainty flower to sway and dance upon the rock. Mom would love this. In all of creation, nothing could make her gasp and smile quicker than seeing flowers. She had books on gardening and houseplants and several on wildflowers. She couldn't grow anything very well, but she could identify them all by name. And if she didn't recognize one, she would search the pages until she found it.

Our last project together was landscaping her yard, and our favorite outing was going to the nursery where we would lose ourselves for hours within the immense bouquet of floral beauty. That thought brought a grin to my lips, and I could almost hear her voice pleading, "Don't cry, sweet one. I am finally home. No more temporary. No more setbacks. No more pain. And oh! Just wait until you see my garden!"

My mother was known on earth as Iris June. Aptly named as one of God's special "wildflowers". When I think about the missed opportunities to explore, to discover the depths of this delightful woman beyond the role she so faithfully played as my mother, I am undone!

Authentic Connection

It doesn't matter what kind of relationship it is. Whether it is a marriage, our biological family members, or friends, it is a frightening thought that we could possibly miss out on one of the greatest gifts our Creator-Relater has ever bestowed on us—heart to heart connection. The desire to be deeply known, to be fully accepted and loved unconditionally, is written within our human DNA. And the One who created us has every intention of fulfilling those innate desires when we are in relationship with Him. The way He loves us changes us. We become empowered with the courage needed to humbly admit that we need help to learn to love well.

When we take a risk and plant ourselves within the sometimes rocky terrain of growing in relationship with other imperfect humans, and if there is to be a life-giving connection, all parties have to be willing to become like that wildflower. Vulnerability is not for the proud or faint of heart! To be open and exposed can appear weak or frail or even foolish by some. But in reality, it becomes the source of rich nutrients feeding the tenacious root system desperately needed for any relationship to become resilient, healthy and rock solid. Being kind but honest is a risk worth taking. Learning the skills to communicate, asking powerful questions and listening well creates the fertile soil that fosters honor and respect. Ah! And then there is the mercy and forgiveness piece. Intimacy and friendship cannot exist without it.

Instead of texting, let's learn to talk. Instead of screen time, let's have playtime. Let's cultivate being deeply connected. Instead of being busy, let's take time and notice what others would not see. Let's be *the hidden ones, the faithful ones, the willing ones.* Being human and learning to love like my mother is a glorious thing. Glory is always attached to sacrifice which is just what love does. Let's learn from the wildflowers around us and become...

So unique, so rare, so worthy!

Leaning In:

- How satisfied are you with your current connections?
- What does being vulnerable look like for you?
- Who is the "wildflower" in your life?
- What is one small step that you could take to show your appreciation to a "hidden one?"

Look at all the beautiful flowers of the field. They don't work or toil, and yet not even Solomon in all his splendor was robed in beauty more than one of these! So if God has clothed the meadow with hay, which is here for such a short time and then dried up and burned, won't he provide for you...

(Matthew 6:28-30, TPT)

3

THE LONGING

AUTHENTIC OR COUNTERFEIT?

I never tire of entering the fantasy world created by Walt Disney. Being driven by a long-held dream and his artistic, creative imagination, his vision of building a theme park became a reality in 1954. His motto, "Believe, dream, dare, do", carries the weight of an anointing that gifted him as a man of vision, one that I believe was provided by the Master Dreamer. I'm inspired by the values undergirding his ability to persevere and risk investing millions to see this dream unfold. Walt opened Disneyland with the following, now famous, words:

> To all who come to this happy place: Welcome. Disneyland is your land. Here age relives fond memories of the past ... and here youth may savor the challenge and promise of the future. Disneyland is dedicated to the ideals, the dreams and the hard facts which have created America ... with the hope that it will be a source of joy and inspiration to all the world. ~ Walt Disney (*Liliane Opsomer* | May 31, 2018. themouseforless.com)

Mom told a story about the first time our family visited Adventureland. There were four of us kids, ranging in ages from two to seven years old. I have no idea how my parents managed to corral four ecstatic, energetic children. But evidently, we weren't the only ones being affected by the magic in the air. At one point, Mom said she looked over at my wide-eyed, grinning father, who was walking down the avenue, unknowingly holding the hand of a child who didn't belong to our family. The little boy's parents were standing next to Mom watching as Dad glanced down at the same time the little guy looked up. Horrified, they both dropped their hand, wheeled around in a moment of desperation, searching for their families. Fortunately for all, the adults were close by and were thoroughly enjoying watching the innocent encounter between the two bewildered, "boys." They called their son, Dad rejoined Mom, everyone had a great laugh and then we all went on our merry way.

As an adult, a huge part of the fascination for me is experiencing the genius of this fairyland existence, which is Disney's ability to weave the fake amidst the real. Most of the landscape is very much alive, including the hill of petunias planted in the shape of Mickey Mouse. Exotic flowers and trees thrive alongside the concrete banks of man-made rivers and lakes. Which ones are real? Only by examining closely can the artificial plants be detected.

Every creature imaginable, from stuffed birds to bionic dinosaurs, come alive as their computerized voices are created and amplified over the loudspeakers, leaving every guest spellbound. Here, for just a moment, a door swings wide, allowing the elderly and the young to enter in and play. Instead of being silenced, all are invited to scream and laugh in hysteria until the tears flow. This is a place that encourages us to dream, daring us to break loose from our limited reality and fly. Here, we experience a world where just for a few minutes, songs of the heart rise to the forefront, and reason and logic take a back seat. Here, the childlike heart is embraced, and the blessing of friends and family is acknowledged. Clean, wholesome fun creates a safe haven for all. Even adults, like my dad, who know better, seem to enjoy being pulled into this surreal adventurous land.

Ah, there it is again! The flutter of excitement. In the mist—a Divine-sent memory. A reminder, a dream of a life that could have been. That should have been in Paradise. The longing to return, to be fully alive in Eden keeps pulling me in!

But the "wonderful World of Disney" is still just that—a make-believe place powered by machines. Mountains and many trees are, in reality, concrete. And moving images on a screen are nothing more than projected waves of light. In the moment, the fantasy captivates us. It is stimulating and satisfying, but only as long as we are under its spell. Granted, everyone knows that Disneyland is a "magical kingdom." Mr. Disney's dream was to entertain his audience, and he was a huge success. However, something happens in me the moment I step off the tram and reenter the parking structure. At first, I feel like I am sinking, like something is dragging me back into a place that I don't want to go. Got to get my feet back onto the ground. Time to return, to grow up and be productive. Time to reenter the *real* world.

Hooked on Peace

Some of my most treasured memories are of our family exploring roads that took us off of the beaten path. We would wake up in our cozy tent early in the morning to the smell of coffee and bacon cooking on the open fire. I loved fishing with my dad, especially when he baited the hook. But I don't think it was so much the experience of fishing that "hooked" me on boating and camping. It was more a magnetic pull from the increasing sense of peace and freedom, the joy of being so far removed from the static of normal existence. Perhaps it was the absence of TV, school and all the demanding voices, or maybe it was just the quiet that would begin to unravel me.

Buzzing insects, harmonizing birds and the crisp fresh air seemed electrically charged, filling me with waves of energy and the boldness to venture out into the unknown. The warming sun would invite me to sit at the edge of each gushing river or glistening lake. I would dangle my tiny feet into the cool water as it gave its greatest performance, skipping and leaping, dancing upon the moving surface, creating illusions of diamonds and painting pastel rainbows just for me.

I remember hiking in the rugged mountainous terrain and hearing a cry in the distance from two glorious eagles. To me, they seemed like appointed guardian angels watching over the deer grazing in the meadow. Ever so often the wind would gently caress my face and fill my lungs with a scent of evergreens that enraptured me.

This was blissful heaven! What a refreshing gift from God. He was there. Everywhere I turned, in every sight, every sound, and every smell. I was created for this—Paradise. No yard, no fences, no streets—just the open expanse of pristine beauty. Life! Thrilling abundance was beckoning me to come and drink my fill of the intoxicating pleasure of sharing these precious moments with Him and my family. If only we could stay. I never wanted to return home. I think He was smiling and feeling the same way.

These holidays always aroused a passionate craving for another life. Curious thoughts, probing questions entered my mind, and a holy dissatisfaction began to tickle my soul. Now, as an adult, I can finally attempt to put words to what I felt. Somehow these experiences had a higher purpose than just vacationing. A relentless hunger was being released within my being. An appreciation and longing for truth was being deposited within my spiritual DNA. This was way beyond just having mental knowledge, studying theology, memorizing Bible verses or having the ability to debate philosophy. Rather, there was a seeking, driving fire that consumed my soul, a thirst for meaningful, authentic, relational connection. I ached for a full life which can only be fulfilled by walking with the Godhead. No counterfeit existence could ever satisfy these desires.

Counterfeit Identity

I am intrigued by the word "counterfeit". I did a little research and discovered some interesting synonyms which gave me insight into why in any other context other than Disneyland I feel so disturbed. Words like bogus, copied, faked, false, forged, fraudulent, phony, crock, imitation, misleading, mock all carry a twisted cruelty, and the end deliverable is a disappointment which bites with a vengeance. Any time we put our faith or hope in an object or especially a person, trusting that they are the "real deal", only to discover that we have been duped, the betrayal we feel can be devastating. The truth is, there is an obscure, counterfeiting operation impacting every single one of us on a daily basis.

I used to associate the concept of a counterfeit with money or art, but of late I have been dwelling on the travesty of loss embraced by the majority of the world who will never know the excitement and fulfillment of stepping into their God-breathed identity and destiny. Sadly, even within the religious world, most will settle into a spectator existence completely unaware that they were created for so much more than to complacently watch someone else live the fantasy life that they wish they had. No wonder there is so much rage and anger consuming and compromising our humanity.

We act so confident that our understanding is complete, that we know for certain the difference between fact and fiction. I have observed some whose opinions are expressed with such controlling force and wrath, that the air is completely sucked out of the relational atmosphere! I find myself asking—Is this reality LIFE? Is this the God-spoken essence of the dream that He had in His heart when He created us, to make man in His image?

But what if? What if within the depths, deep below the brilliant vision of men like Walt Disney, the Presence of Holy Inspiration is there, longing to captivate us? What if He is delighting in the prospect of introducing and attuning our senses to experience Him in HIS world, to hear beyond and recognize His voice and the quiet melodies of His songs? I find myself drifting into lyrics that move me, melodies pregnant with hope pass through me and mysteriously become part of me. For a split second, I sense something beyond this physical me. It is spiritual, as if the whole of my being is a timeless song written by the Perfect Composer who has been singing over me since before I was formed in my mother's womb. Each note is a sound that explodes into a refraction of light, like millions of gemstones reflecting the Image of His pure beauty. What if we were created for this realm which pulsates with Life, Who indeed is a Person offering a Way to live in Truth which is immersed in kindness and gentleness? What if He longs to be one with us?

It is difficult to find words that adequately describe what I sense in these fleeting moments. Scripture describes my present frustration adequately. *Now we see things imperfectly, like puzzling reflections in a mirror, but then we will see everything with perfect clarity. All that I know now is partial and incomplete, but then I will know everything completely, just as God now knows me completely.* (1 Corinthians 13:12, NLT)

Could it be that Walt Disney was inspired to create a world of fantasy that gives us a glimpse into the real spiritual life that God had in mind for us all along? Doesn't He encourage us to expect the unexpected? Hasn't the Father of mankind made us in His image with the potential for genius, to think and imagine impossible things becoming real? Is He not the composer of every musical score, and the Author of the greatest story ever told?

The mystery and intrigue revealing the story of Jesus embody all of the classic themes that stir our hearts and draw us into the plot. It has it all—angels and demons, supernatural virgin birth, symphonies of worship, heroes and villains, good versus evil, divine intervention, fleeing from murderous kings, hiding and escape, and a surprising happy ending! This heavenly narrative continually overshadows and defies scientific law and earthly wisdom and ushers in a whole new paradigm for existence.

Scene after scene reveals the passionate heart and character of our Champion, Jesus, the promised Messiah, the only Son of God, clothed in flesh, living as an ordinary carpenter. His life ministry disrupts the status quo of a corrupt tradition long held by the Jewish leaders, and day after day His radical teachings and actions display the miraculous as the newly established norm for His faithful followers. The Son of Man's compassion for the sinner exposes the heartless facade of religious law and piety, the most heinous demonic counterfeit of all! In the end, we watch God demonstrate authentic love as the Sacrificial Lamb of God surrenders His life, carrying the weight of sin from the cross to the grave. We are left awestruck to discover that His cruel death was not the final chapter, but instead the opening of a new book.

The curse that overshadowed God's most treasured creation—mankind—was finally broken. A new era, a new Kingdom was ushered in, allowing anyone who believes to enter, not just His story, but His family. We are now invited in as sons and daughters, and all who choose to worship and sing His song are truly flowing in full assurance, building the harmonic cadence which is destined to perfectly resolve into Life eternal. Together, in Christ, we have been written and flow within the musical score, the resurrected song which originated within the Father heart of God before the world began. It was a world without sin and pain, without bondage and fear. In the beginning, His was a perfect world, an existence of perfect harmony.

Dare to Imagine

What is this insatiable desire within me? How do I describe it? What is this impulse that seems to come from beyond, beckoning me to seek that which I have not known before? Is it God? It is a fragrance that arouses my senses and excites the curiosity of the child which still exists within my adult being. I am compelled to search, and I am so eager to learn. I continue to wait. I long to know the fulness of this mysterious, fantastic Person and experience LIFE!

God is drawing us all back to Himself. I believe that there is an invitation from the Father to dare to imagine the unthinkable. But for that to happen, we must allow Him to break our locked-in thinking. His desire is to teach us to think in new ways, to tap into His realm of possibilities which is limitless. There is a future full of the hope of unexpected freedom, boundless, expansive, timeless change—never arriving at completion because eternity is unending and so is our potential! I believe there is a window opening within the spiritual heavenly realm where creative secrets are being poured out into the minds and hearts of those who are quietly seeking. What if you and I have been prepared vessels to receive these timely inspirational nuggets? What if when these gifts are expressed, whether it is in writing, or art, on film, in music or dance, the end result will draw seekers into an experience of truth, releasing an anointed, explosive awareness of the Presence and Majesty of Jesus? It's time for us all to reflect on the vital issues of life!

So, what about you? If it's true that each of us is an image-bearer of the infinite Creator, and every soul is uniquely designed to carry different aspects of God's DNA, then what has He placed in you? In you alone!? What unique potential genius dwells within you? If all the fear were stripped away, if you were allowed to grow in a perfect environment of love, in an atmosphere where you could dream and there was no possibility to fail, where there was no criticism, only encouragement, what could you imagine? Dare to imagine the unthinkable!

Leaning In:

- What are you believing about yourself that has become locked-in thinking?
- What creates excitement and passion within you?
- What is keeping you from being authentic?
- What can you identify in your life that might be counterfeit?
- What attributes characterize your authentic self?

I pray with great faith for you, because I'm fully convinced that the One who began this glorious work in you will faithfully continue the process of maturing you and will put his finishing touches to it until the unveiling of our Lord Jesus Christ.
(Philippians 1:6, TPT)

4

TURKEY IN ASIA

DELICIOUS PERSEVERANCE

Have you ever felt homesick? Ever been separated from your family and miss them so much that there is a literal throbbing ache in your gut? Ever felt utter desperation? The kind that drives you to act in "unreasonable" ways? Ever loved someone so much that you would do anything—*anything*— to show them, to convince them, to demonstrate to them just how much you care? Well, that would be me! I was completely caught off guard as to what an adventurous move around the globe would entail.

In 1984, my husband and I sold everything we owned and headed for full-time missions. So much for the mundane and normal! After spending a year in training through Youth with a Mission, we finally arrived in Hong Kong. Leaving home and stepping into Asia was surreal. It was like being baptized in a river of exotic Eastern potpourri. The spice of China was fascinating. Fragrant oil of ancient history permeated the present day and mixed with the flow of everyday life. Mythical superstitions inspired artists to paint and sculpt dragons and these scary demonized creatures stood guard at the entrance of parks and public buildings. The forefathers were anything but dead. A woodsy scent of musk filled the smoky air originating from incense lit by the masses as they bowed to the age-old traditions of ancestral worship. Altars were erected in many homes and businesses, displaying the daily offerings.

China was truly a land of contrasts. Sweet and sour. The collision of opposites! We visited ornate Buddhist temples laden with golden statues standing alone in the quiet, serene countryside as well as congested cities built around gray concrete high-rise apartments. Wading through the ongoing stream of coal black-haired bicyclists, we joined the rushing crowds on foot, jamming into buses and trains. Exhaust fumes engulfed the overcrowded streets burning our eyes and lungs. Neon signs flashed unrecognizable words made of weird-looking lines and symbols above every shop. Chopsticks replaced forks, and instead of eggs and pancakes for breakfast, we were served rice and tasty chicken's feet.

The mesmerizing music of the Orient was captivating. Vocalists with a nasally whine sang peculiar melodies created from dissonant chords. The musical notes seemed to rise and fall even within their language, especially in the open market place as merchants argued about prices with their customers. Terraced rice fields carved out of mountainous terrain covered parts of the country like exquisite, vibrant green patchwork quilts. Oxen pulled carts and plows, and elderly men and women struggled beneath the weight of heavy baskets. We entered rural villages, where barefoot children dressed in rags rushed to greet us with sparkling eyes and smiles that would melt your heart.

So began the journey to discover our new normal. My goal, especially for my children, was to make the transition into this new culture easier by continuing to celebrate our American holidays. The challenge I decided to give myself was to find a way to surprise my family with a traditional American meal on our first Thanksgiving Day.

"Mom, Where's the Turkey?"

At home in the States, much of my everyday routine revolved around the planning, preparation, serving and clean-up of meals. My fully-loaded kitchen was probably the most important room in the house. For me, every appliance was an essential that I took for granted, at least until I no longer had them. Try to survive without a stove and oven, a refrigerator, without a dishwasher or a washer and dryer for a few days, and you will enter a culture shock of your own! My large beautiful kitchen was history, and so was shopping at big American supermarkets.

Every day my children and I walked to the open market. I think it's called the open market because everything is sold on the street and nothing is packaged. Instead of a steak in a nice clean wrapper, I had to select from chunks of flesh covered with flies hanging from hooks. Baskets of snakes and other slithering delicacies were constantly being offered to me by smiling Chinese merchants. I think they enjoyed seeing the horror in our eyes. And the smells! There is no way to describe the open market aroma. Let's just say that I had to fight "tossing my cookies" on a daily basis.

I stood in the small 5'x5' room, which was a standard Chinese kitchen, and looked around. A shallow counter held my one-burner hot plate, the electric skillet and my wok. I also had a new crockpot. That's it! It would have to do.

I had to get closer to the main part of the city in Hong Kong where most Westerners lived. Surely, I could find a market that would cater to foreigners. Traveling by train for an hour, we finally arrived in Hong Kong and found a store that actually had rows of food on shelves. I was thrilled to see familiar items, with brand names in English. Everything was expensive, but it didn't matter. It was almost Thanksgiving Day, and I was on a mission. My kids wanted turkey.

I turned the corner with my shopping cart and stood breathlessly before the frozen food section. My eyes began to scan the freezer. Under my breath, I prayed, "Please let there be a turkey. Please let there be a turkey."

And there he was. The Butterball himself! I wanted to grab the frozen bird to my chest and break into a jig, but some women had already begun to gather around my cart, pointing at the bird and laughing at me. I guess to them, we Americans looked as strange as the oversized chicken riding in my cart!

I returned home with a smile on my face and renewed determination in my heart. Now! How was I going to get that bird into my crock-pot? It was obvious that it wasn't going to fit without some kind of surgery. After a good defrosting, I took the largest knife I had and began the operation. If I could just cut it in half, it would work.

It didn't sound like an impossible task, but as the hour passed, the dull knife began to cause blisters to form on my hands. I couldn't do it! I was just not strong enough, and my knife was too dull. I began to pray through the tears, "Please help me. I can't do this on my own."

There is a stubbornness that runs in my family. I am not a quitter. That day I began to learn something about perseverance. God did not stop my hands from blistering. He did not immediately answer my prayer and transform my knife into a supercharged chainsaw cutting through the bone of that turkey. (How amazing would that have been!) After a few more hours of hard laboring, I finally produced an American Thanksgiving meal. Believe me, everything inside of my being wanted to sacrifice that turkey as a burnt offering on our fire pit. At times I felt like throwing it! Stomping on it! Anything but cooking it! But seeing the delight in my children's eyes at the table that evening made the whole experience worth it.

Here is a remarkable quality about our Father that I am beginning to understand. It appears to me that from His higher-ways-perspective-and-priorities, rather than showing off His miracle-making skills, most often He seems to enjoy enabling us to become *super* in our *natural*, which is exactly what we step into when we choose to not quit under pressure! He loves it when we share our deepest desires with Him and confidently trust in our relationship that He hears and answers. I find that His gracious way of answering prayer is either correcting what I am asking for (especially when I am overcome by a spirit of stupid!) or He takes great liberty and the Giver of every perfect gift offers me far more than I ask for, sometimes in quantity but most often in quality. And that gift is usually packaged in a beautifully wrapped process that carries a lifetime guarantee. I am growing in my relationship with my Creator, and each encounter is building experiential knowledge and understanding of His ways which are absolutely out of this world! Higher! Better! Totally mysterious! There is nothing comparable to the surprises that await when you knock on the doors He leads you to explore.

You might ask, "What was the big deal? Why even ask for a turkey? Why bother seeking a turkey in a foreign land? Why didn't you just give up and serve chicken stir fry over rice?"

Well, culture, traditions, and holidays had all been just words. Until now, I had never given a thought to the significance of my heritage. I had been swallowed up by the mundane normal existence of an American lifestyle. We were truly blessed to live in the United States, a country of such wealth. All of our modern conveniences really did make life easier. But they also enabled us to keep up with our self-inflicted stressful lifestyle. We honestly believed that there was no other way to live. I adopted the microwave mentality—quick-acting, immediate gratification. My life was spinning, and the setting was on high. My soul was becoming dry and overcooked until Mercy finally pushed the cancel button and removed me from the soul-blistering, spiritdrying oven of my over-committed, hurried way of life, and I now had a choice—give up or persevere.

Thankful Roots

In my culture, Thanksgiving Day is a holy day; at least it used to be. It is a special day to remember our roots, to celebrate courage and commitment. It is a day to honor our forefathers and their desire and determination to have a new way of life, but first and foremost, it is a day set aside to reflect on the substance of their spirit.

They arrived in America with a faith in God that was as raw and bountiful as the wild, new frontier which drew and challenged them. Hope was so real and utterly compelling that they could not stop until they found a home. Their dream of living in freedom was birthed and empowered by the Master Dreamer Himself.

I believe I understand what sustained our pioneering parents in their search for a new world. They had been touched by the bloodied hands of a loving Son Who truly knows what it is to ache for home. The only Son of God left heaven to become one of us, and He not only felt the intensity of His own homesickness, but He was kind enough to identify with ours. These courageous ones had been inspired by the only One Who truly has experienced the full extent of our ravaging hunger and thirst and sickness! This Savior knows the agony of carrying the bodies of His beloved into the grave.

Our forefathers were captivated by His love and a dream which produced a joy that was so resilient that even death couldn't touch it. To our parents, the journey of finding home began by returning. Returning, not to the place of their birth, but to a cross, the place prepared for their rebirth. It was here, in the light of sacrifice, that Love was defined and given a Face. The smile of forgiveness, the blessing of total and unconditional acceptance and the freedom to just BE defines home pretty well, don't you think? This is what drove our founding fathers to rebel against religious tyranny and find a place, a land where they could live out what they had already discovered in their hearts. Home! Worth living for! For many, worth dying for!

I guess if you were to ask me why I was so unrelenting that Thanksgiving Day, my answer would be—because deep down I am an American woman, and the faith of our mothers is still very much alive and kicking within my own heart. I, too, have been touched by the merciful Hands of heaven. They continually prompt me to express my affection in countless ways, some of which are more painful than others. And I was a bit homesick. My will is always very much engaged in the demonstration of my devotion to God and to those whom I love. But let's face it, when it gets tough and bloody, it is only because God's will is imprinted on our will that we are able to truly love at all.

Love is the powerful force behind perseverance! It's the courageous energy that is capable of launching our tenacious spirits into the unknown realms of what's possible. And the wonder of it all is that from the beginning of time, the relentless Love of God set a course to intercept our hearts so that we have a perpetual filling station. He fills. He fuels our fortitude. Spirit to spirit, His Almighty strength is made available to us so that difficulties can be overcome with "great and honorable actions." ~ *William Bradford*

When we are given and receive faith, desperation can be transformed into determination. In my story, I asked for a turkey, stepped out in faith, went on a wild-turkey-chase and God answered. I received it. I asked for help, and He downloaded grace to persevere. Frustration given to our Father can become fuel for fruitfulness. This is a supernova, glorious partnership! When the pressures of our life want to squeeze the life right out of us, Jesus has this creative ability to cause those very stressors to work for us.

If we draw close to Him and engage Him in those difficult moments, we will witness an explosion of strength, a colorful array of brilliant strategies to overcome, excel and be victorious. We become His supernova masterpiece!

I wonder what our Promise Keeper is encouraging you to lean into, to *ask, seek, and knock*? What is He prompting within you which will open the doorway of faith into His willingness to hear and answer, *it shall be given, you will find, it will be open to you*? What is this experiential Partnership worth to you? Is it valuable enough to push you past your fear and pain into laboring for it? Because fortifying any meaningful relationship requires work. I ask this because I now understand that the true Treasure, the Blessing within our journey, is Him! Walking with Him, talking with Him and of course, the doing aspects—both the shared, significant exploits as well as the mundane, everyday living part as well.

I am so very grateful. For all of it—For my faithful Father who is a merciful God, for the kindness of His Son who left home to rescue me, for the Spirit living within my faith-driven Pilgrim parents and myself, and yes... for the turkey and the crockpot. I was and will forever be... truly thankful!

Leaning In:

- What does perseverance look like to you in your current circumstances?
- What pressures are you facing that are attempting to squeeze the life out of you?
- What can you do to position yourself to receive the strength and fortitude that is available to you from your Father?
- If you envision the perfect outcome for your situation, what would that look like?
- What obstacles stand in the way of your vision coming true?

It was answered, all great and honourable actions are accompanied with great difficulties, and must be both enterprised and overcome with answerable courages. It was granted ye dangers were great, but not desperate; the difficulties were many, but not invincible... and all of them, through ye help of God, by fortitude and patience, might either be borne, or overcome.

(*"Of Plymouth Plantation" by WILLIAM BRADFORD, 1647*)

5

500 SQUARE FEET

THE COST OF FALSE CONTENTMENT

They called us the white devils. We arrived by train from Hong Kong to the village of Fanling, and everywhere we went our blond hair and hazel eyes drew attention. Living on the island of Hong Kong, there were many Westerners, but we were now moving an hour away from the city where some of the locals had never ventured out of the village. To them, we were strangers, foreigners and a threat. For many, fear was their master, and their only place of refuge was found behind the barred doors and windows of their homes.

Prior to the move, our family had been staying at the Hong Kong Youth with a Mission (YWAM) base as missionaries. Our training through YWAM was supposed to prepare us for culture shock. As Americans, we came with an inbred set of standards, traditions and mindsets. We were not there as tourists. In our hearts, we were there to stay. This meant a radical death to many of our Western ways and especially our Yankee pride. Every day we were reminded that we were aliens. I thought we were actually coping pretty well, but after a few months of living in the extremely cramped, one-room accommodations at the base, the thought of a possible real home with more space and no mold sounded like heaven to me. Our desire was to move out of Hong Kong into New Territories, and this appeared to be God's answer to our cry for provision.

Fanling was a typical Chinese village, a gloomy gray concrete maze connected by hundreds of dark, narrow alleys. Every building was at least three stories high. We were the first Westerners to ever be allowed to live inside their village. Erick, a young Chinese student who was being mentored by my husband, led us here. His father was one of the chief elders of the village and the owner of several homes. One just happened to be vacant. After much persuasion, he had convinced his dad to allow us to rent from them.

We followed Erick walking single-file to our new home, stepping over garbage and dodging the rats in the gutters. The old women stared at us with angry scowls. No welcome wagon here! A lump began to form in my throat as my hope for an American home and lifestyle shattered. I plastered a fake smile on my face as Erick stopped and unlocked the door to the apartment that would be our new dwelling place.

We entered through the kitchen. A huge brick fire pit holding an enormous wok had blackened the tile walls with smoke and grease. There were no cabinets. A thin counter held a hot-plate and in the corner by the door was a miniature sink. Off of the kitchen was a tiny bathroom with a child-size bathtub that would also be used as my washing machine in the days to come and a small sink. To my shock and delight, instead of the traditional hole in the floor, known as the "squatty-potty", there was a real western-style toilet.

Up the first set of stairs, there were two narrow bedrooms and a shallow cove between the two rooms that became our dining room. Up another flight of stairs, we entered the living room and another little bedroom. Every window peered into the privacy of the neighboring houses. The last stairway led to the flat roof where the clothesline was strung. Incredible! We had a whole 500 square feet of house connected by three flights of stairs. We were all dripping with sweat by the time we reached the roof.

As the tour ended, Erick explained a few rules that his father expected us to obey. The main living room downstairs, off the kitchen, was the dwelling place of the family dynasty and we were never to enter the sacred shrine. In addition, Erick's mother had an altar erected in the kitchen and once a day she would enter the house to light incense and bring her offering, usually a piece of fruit. This would ensure the family prosperity and health and appease the wrath of the ancestors. For some Chinese, the ancestors are viewed as gods that must be honored and worshipped.

A Wakeup Call

On the morning of our first day in Fanling, we were awakened at four AM by a series of blasts, like that of a rapid-firing machine gun. After peeling myself off the ceiling and comforting my frightened children, we came to find they were firecrackers. In Asia, firecrackers play an important role in their everyday religious experience. They light them constantly as part of any celebration. They are also used as a weapon in spiritual warfare to frighten off "evil spirits". In the States, I had many fond memories of celebrating Independence Day. Watching fireworks and hearing firecrackers explode in the distance was all part of the excitement and fun, but in a foreign country at four AM, not so much! I wish I could tell you that my response was an immediate, self-controlled prayer, blessing my enemies. At that point, I was more like the apostolic sons of thunder wanting to pray down the consuming fire of God on my adversaries! This ritual became our new alarm clock. It took weeks for my nerves to settle and months for the Lord to soften and convict my raging heart.

It wasn't just the ongoing blast of the infuriating explosives. There was no place to go within our house that was quiet. Every noise, every voice, every screaming mother and crying child could be heard through our walls. At night the racket continued with the addition of a loud clicking sound coming from a game that everyone played using tiles, something like our Dominoes. This went on into the wee hours of the morning. During these days of transition, the temperature was over 100°F with the humidity factor soaring in the high 90s. It felt like we were living on a perpetual Stair Master, and we had no air conditioning. My nerves were fried. My strength was sapped, and all I wanted to do was curl up in a ball and hide under my sheets. I had a bad attitude, and this was as close to hell as I ever wanted to get!

I will never forget the morning I awoke and literally stumbled downstairs to cook breakfast, smacking my toe on the concrete stairs. I limped across the kitchen to open the front door in an attempt to find even a breath of cool air. There were no screens on the doors or windows. Soon after beginning breakfast, I turned from my eggs just in time to see two Chinese women step through my door. They stood in the kitchen, pointing and laughing and babbling on and on in Cantonese. I just smiled and said, "Sure, come on in. Check it all out."

After they did a thorough investigation of the kitchen and bathroom, they bowed, waved and said in perfect English, "Goodbye." Stunned, I turned back to my overcooked eggs, silenced a giggle and whispered, "I can't believe this!"

In that moment the reality of our cultural differences really hit home. Literally! Privacy and having my own space around my body and in my home was a non-negotiable American standard and comfort zone. We were taught to knock and wait to be invited into another's house. We were instructed not to violate other's airspace. But here it seemed as if there was no such teaching. Every day I was confronted and challenged by this new culture. The glamour and excitement of being a missionary was gone, and I wanted out. I wallowed in self-pity for months. Why did Jesus seem so far away and why wasn't He helping me to cope? Where was His grace? Jesus did answer, but it came in a very unexpected way.

One afternoon I left the kids with my husband and went out for a walk. At the edge of town, I discovered a well-worn path leading away from the village and winding into the lush tropical countryside. Except for the bantering between a pair of strange-looking bugs, it was quiet. Stepping into silence muffled the relentless chatter within my mind. I stopped and sank into the depths of the tranquil stillness. My prayer forced its way to the surface like a diver coming up for air. "I am so sorry," I prayed. "I have not done very well adjusting to all of this. It's just been incredibly difficult!"

Up the trail entangled within a thick, century-old vine, I happened to notice a shack built out of old rotten pieces of scrap wood and metal. There was no glass in the window, and inside a woman sat on the dirt floor. Her bare feet and torn dress and especially the sadness in her eyes pierced my heart.

"Difficult is always relative, isn't it?"

His kind and gentle voice gripped my heart as I stared at the woman. Her dark hollow eyes still disturb me to this day.

"Self-pity blinds you." Jesus' soft voice continued deep in my soul, lifting my eyes off of my own pain. *"You create your own reality, and it locks you into a miserable existence without Me."*

His words burned. He was right. I repented and asked for His strength and grace. I knew I needed His heart to love these people and their culture as He did. Something deep in me shifted, and I returned to my house with an entirely new perspective. Compared to this woman's dwelling, it now felt like a palace. I scrubbed every inch of it until it shined and began to decorate it in my mind. When I looked at it through this new lens, I knew that if this was God's plan for me, I could stay there for the rest of my life.

A Rare Discovery

Sometimes our Heavenly Father's compassionate provision arrives in curious packages. I find His loving ways extremely uncomfortable and a bit puzzling. I am hopeful that I won't always be in spiritual culture shock. Because I am His child and heaven-bound, He is faithful to discipline and train me. He answered my prayer for a home, but His solution to my dilemma was ordained to reveal my deeper need. My entrenched American mindset and expectations were controlling my reactions to many of life's situations. I was bound and imprisoned by these. It's not until you leave your own country and are immersed in another that the impact of this reality is truly felt.

Finding genuine contentment is a rare treasure. For me, the search began with a revelation and a repentant heart. It was Jesus who heard my cry for help. In His mercy, He led me down a path to a shack, to a young tattered Chinese woman alone in a dirty hut. How easily I forget who I am and where I am going. I forget that everything in my comfortable world is only temporary. I am so rich in earthly blessings. And yet, if I'm not careful my spirit starves and begins to dwell in a dirty hovel like hers.

To enter the realm of God's existence, I must embrace flexibility. I don't really care for stretching! But to remain rigid and unbending is to resist His hand, which is forever rescuing me from the messes I create as I attempt to be god. It's painful! My stubborn will would rather be the potter. Let someone else be the clay! He delights in infinite variety. I don't! I prefer the comfort of the familiar. Sameness is easier and less stressful. His inexpressible beauty can be found within every person in every nation. I know this is true, but I really need help to see what is not always obvious. I guess, in a way, life in God surpasses culture. Perhaps His desire is to touch the world through a chosen people who will express godliness in the fullness of diversity. What does that look like? I can only imagine!

We don't always get to choose where we live on this earth, but when it comes to our spiritual dwelling place, it is ours for the taking. In Fanling, I had 500 square feet. When my heart embraced it with thankfulness, gratitude led me to contentment, and peace began to transform our little house into a home.

I wonder how many of us feel like aliens where we are, even if we live in our own home country? If you examine your inner thoughts, where do you feel discontented? What needs to change externally? An even more powerful question is what is your Counselor highlighting in your heart that needs an overhaul? Where do you need a perspective upgrade? What if you were on the brink of having a massive breakthrough, where you were being invited to step beyond your map into a heavenly dimension of revelation; one that would alter your lens, giving you 20/20 vision to see, understanding, and the ability to interpret life from a completely new and heavenly vantage point? What would you do? I ask this because if I'm really honest, even after returning to America, I still sometimes feel out of place. It feels like Someone has been tampering with my head and heart. The familiar has lost its fizz! What used to be of major importance in the here and now has become minor pettiness in light of thereafter. Maybe true contentment finds a permanent home in our hearts when we are comfortable being a bit uncomfortable living in our skin. Maybe it means knowing that the misfits that we are in the present will only fit completely someday, and the reason that our spirits feel displaced today, is because they are. And that is okay. Let's walk-off our map. Let's take responsibility for our thoughts, say YES to change and explore the secrets that await as we step into the Faith Frontier!

Leaning In:

- What does contentment look like for you?

- What are three things you can identify which might be blessings in disguise?
- What are you learning now that could be vital to your future destiny?
- Where do you need the Lord's perspective in your current struggle?
- How can you tap into His wisdom and truth?

I know what it means to lack, and I know what it means to experience overwhelming abundance. For I'm trained in the secret of overcoming all things, whether in fullness or in hunger. And I find that the strength of Christ's explosive power infuses me to conquer every difficulty.
(*Philippians* 4:12-13, *TPT*)

6

THE DIRTY WINDOW

BEAUTY BEYOND

My aunt says that I was a rather solemn child growing up. Beneath the surface of my everyday ordinary existence, there was a subterranean surging reality. From the depths, an endless stream of thoughts and questions surfaced like a hidden spring seeping into my consciousness. I don't remember being sad, just bashful and pensive. My introverted pondering left me feeling a bit quirky and usually nervous in the presence of my other outgoing peers.

Church was a huge part of our young lives. We were fed a steady diet of Bible stories, hymns and the infamous church potlucks. Usually, the announcement of a visiting missionary was met with the rolling of eyes and a groan from the kids. Bored and restless, the bulletin became our saving grace. Elaborately folding the sheet of weekly announcements, the boys competed to see who could create the coolest jet. The girls used the time to write and sneak notes to one another. As much as I tried to participate in our Pony Express under-pew operation, I was constantly distracted by the missionary's stories and the interesting pictures of native children that lit up the wall in front of me. Somehow, those slides rolled right off the screen and into my heart.

Over the years, a growing desire to enter their world would randomly appear out of nowhere like lightning, invading my comfortable small universe. Illuminated within the shadowy recesses of my mind was the veiled memory of those nameless faces. A pathway of destiny was revealed. The invitation to follow was extended. And I said, Yes!

The Unveiling

My imagination is a God-given gift to feed my faith. I don't know how to hope without it. As a kid, I spent hours dreaming about being a missionary, trying to imagine what it would be like. My creative, innocent mind traveled to the ends of the earth. It was here that I felt no fear. No insecurity. No restrictions. It was always a perfect world.

As I grew older, those youthful daydreams shaped not only my educational direction but also my marital choice. Now a wife and a mother of two, my childhood longing finally had been fulfilled. I found myself off the pew and around the planet surrounded by a sea of curious faces like those hidden away in my heart as a little girl.

After settling in New Territories, my husband began his marriage and family counseling ministry. In addition to building his practice, he was also training young pastors, and he was gone. A lot! And I ... I was attempting to create a home out of old used furniture and learn to cook strange green vegetables in a wok. I was also teaching my children and attempting to be a supportive wife. Surviving the sweltering heat, the unfamiliar smells, but mostly the loneliness of Hong Kong was my ongoing trial. This was NOT how I had imagined it! The cruel face of raw, painful reality was relentless, pounding away at the doorway of my make-believe world. An eviction notice was issued to my childish gullibility. Over the years, disappointment and disillusionment began to vie for space where innocent joy once resided. Asia became my pressure cooker. There was no way out. And I was being tenderized!

We had recently moved out of the village of Fanling into a much larger apartment on the outskirts of town. It was just one of those days—you know, where you wake up feeling exhausted, overwhelmed and irritated. I felt overworked and unappreciated. I stood at the living room window and as I peered through the glass, my eyes settled on the security bars. I felt like a caged animal. I missed my home and my family. I longed for the freedom that comes with living in my own culture and understanding the language. At that moment, loneliness gripped me like a noose around my neck.

Tenderly, Jesus asked, "*Debbie, what do you see?*"

I sighed. "I see an old dirty window with bars covered with chipped paint and mildew." As I described in great detail the window before me, another question entered my mind. This time His question was laced with a hint of excitement.

"*Look beyond the window. Tell me. What do you see?*"

As I peered through the bars, I described the courtyard below. The high humidity formed a natural greenhouse for the thriving emerald jungle surrounding our apartment building. The magnificent wild foliage was unlike anything I had ever seen. There was a circular driveway encasing a neglected lawn. An old metal swing-set made of heavy pipes stood in the middle of the grass. It was the perfect play area for my children.

"*Life is a gift, and every day you have the choice as to whether you will focus on the old dirty window or find the beauty that lies beyond.*" His words were infused with power! I could feel His confidence in me, and the energy of encouragement filled my motivational tank to make the choice to *look beyond.*

Walking It Out

We usually don't recognize the most important moments of our lives; at least, I don't. This simple little gemstone has been a constant companion throughout the years. But honestly, at times it feels more like a rock in my shoe. It takes work to overcome negative feelings and discover the treasures seen only through the eyes of God, especially when I am in distress and hurting. I'm just not good at it!

Over the years I have been given many opportunities to practice the art of *looking beyond*. Homeschooling my children was a great example of this. It was about two years before we left for the mission field. I can't even begin to tell you the angst I felt when the Lord asked me to remove the kids from the Christian School and teach them at home. I absolutely could not understand why He would prompt me to do that. It was an awesome school. I was just beginning to enjoy a bit of freedom as a mom, having a few hours of peace and quiet with them being away at school. I was really resistant to the idea, but I couldn't shake His words. He said, "*I want them set apart! They both are significant in My Kingdom, and I don't want them ruined by the system.*"

The more I processed, the more excited I got. A huge hook for me was Jesus reminding me of the cruel teasing I had experienced from my peers in school and how damaging it was to my self-esteem. I would do just about anything to save them from that trauma!

Fortunately, I really enjoyed being creative, which saved my bacon, especially with Jason because his learning style was very different from the traditional teaching method used in public schools. Being a creative thinker and a hands-on learner myself, I was on my face constantly asking for wisdom and creative ideas.

One night in the middle of the night, I was inspired to create a game to help him with his phonics lesson. I made a template of a large foot print out of construction paper, made a duplicate for each letter of the alphabet, laminated them, cut them out and then printed a capital and lowercase letter onto each foot. Jason was really into guns, so I got him one that would shoot a dart with a rubber tip. I would throw several letters on the floor, make the sound of each letter and he would identify it verbally and shoot the correct letter. Those early years were so enjoyable and rewarding.

But as you can imagine, normal life always has its ups and downs, sick days, cranky days, and the need for all to have some space and time away from each other. I can't tell you the number of times that I had to retreat to my room to silently scream into my pillow! Especially on the mission field! There were certainly moments where my focus was definitely on the chipped paint and mildew. This was a really demanding job! It was a huge sacrifice of my time and energy.

But looking back, the pay-off for both the kids and me was enormous. That experience taught me as much as the kids. I learned to depend on my Great Teacher like never before. The bond that was established between the kids and me would last forever. They were spared a ton of grief by not being exposed to the harsh reality of the negative socialization that happens in public school. Granted, life would definitely throw all of us some painful curve balls in the future, but the fruit in our lives from that decision to homeschool has been a beauty to behold. Both the kids have grown into extraordinary adults, each uniquely gifted and obviously *set apart for Kingdom exploits*!

Looking Beyond

Patience and determination are required to overlook the obvious disarray in my circumstances and especially in people, including myself. Maybe I should use the words reframe or refocus instead of overlook. It is so easy for us to focus on what is dirty or wrong, or what needs to be fixed. I have been told that I have an eye for detail. I am a fixer. It's what I do. I normally don't just look for the negative to complain about it. I see it for what it is—a challenge to be addressed and overcome. When this is in the context of a project, it is a handy gift to have. It really is one of my greatest strengths. But when a person in my inner circle becomes the project, it becomes my greatest weakness. I see the flaws, and if I'm not careful the log in my own eye becomes a battering ram, pulverizing the precious one who I am attempting to help. There are some things in this life that are not ours to correct, even if we could do something about them.

The old nature, which I will call the "fixer, control freak", would love to dominate our reactions on a daily basis and have us dwell in the negative. As followers of Christ, this is where the rubber meets the road. Where are you being called to *look beyond?* The Eyes of Love fixate on all that is good, and right and holy and just. Sight is available for the blind. We have been invited into Kingdom clarity, the ability to rise above any situation and see from God's perspective. What do you see? Being captivated by His view displaces negativity. It fills us with renewed hope which enables us to be carriers of Light. Will we embrace an imperfect world and have the eyes to see beyond the negatives—*the bars and chipped paint*? Will we look for the perfect Image of the Almighty within the brokenness of mankind or will we cling to our short-sighted judgments and opinions? Fortunately, we are not enslaved to that old temperament any longer. Love continues to entice us with the promise of complete joy and freedom from discouragement, giving us the eyes to see. I have decided to choose life. When I cooperate with His process, I am a much happier person.

I will always be a missionary, whether I live in a foreign country or at home. To uncover and magnify the good, not just in circumstances but also in people, is truly my desire. He alone can empower and fulfill this longing within me. He was right. Life is a gift, and our destinies are being walked out one choice at a time, one day at a time. What beauty lies beyond? He knows. He sees... and He shares it. Will we? It will forever be our choice!

Leaning In:

- Where do you feel hopeless and discouraged in your life?
- If you were to look beyond the problem, how do you see the Lord at work?
- What is one choice you could make that would help you gain a higher perspective?
- What are you believing about your future?

So keep your thoughts continually fixed on all that is authentic and real, honorable and admirable, beautiful and respectful, pure and holy, merciful and kind. And fasten your thoughts on every glorious work of God, praising him always.
(Philippians 4:8, TPT)

7

THE CROCUS

WINTER IS ALMOST OVER

Winter was lingering. We had only been home from the mission field for a few months. We were renting a small house up by Mount Hood in Oregon, and I knew no one. I felt so alone and restless. After pacing the floor for what seemed hours, I finally pulled out my snow gear, grabbed my boots and headed outside.

As I walked the streets, an eerie dark cloud crept towards me like a predator stalking its prey. An icy chill shot down my spine. Hazy fog twisted into the shape of long boney fingers gripping a dagger. "Where is your God? How could He let this happen to you?" The hideous misty creature slashed at my mind. "What if there is no God? What if you have committed your life to something that is not real?" Snarling and scoffing, the mocking accusations continued, driving the poisonous blade deeper and deeper into the artery of my faith. "Where is His protection now? If He is so loving, why didn't He stop this from happening?"

Freezing cold air cut through the layers of my clothes, burning my skin, ruthlessly stabbing at every cell of my body. I was falling and spinning and clutching at any shred of truth that would break my fall and ease the pain. But truth seemed to have vanished within the presence of this acidy shadow of death.

As a young woman, one of my greatest desires was to be a wife and mother. At the age of twenty, I married the only man I had ever loved. I was naive and hopeful, and I honestly thought it was possible to live "happily ever after." I believed in marriage. Forever! I thought we both did. I just had no clue how much determination and work it would take to blend our two very fragmented lives. But we had come so far!

The weight of anger attempting to protect my broken heart pressed hard against the knife being thrust into my soul. The image of my husband's face and seventeen years of hazy memories shot through the deepening darkness, slicing and gouging, embedding themselves in my mind like shards of shattered glass. Finally, after weeks of being numb, it was time to succumb and feel the agonizing reality of his betrayal. Excruciating grief hit my stomach and at last, the suppressed anguish fueling my anger broke loose. The avalanche of sorrow hit. My shaking hands grabbed for my knees. Gasping for air, my whole body began to convulse as a silent scream of rage surrendered, giving way to deep gut-wrenching sobs.

"There is no God, and you are alone." The hateful presence brushed against my neck, sending another shudder down my back.

Being lost is a very frightening experience. I was stumbling through a hellish maze in a pitch-blackness that only exists where there is no God. The wicked voices violate your psyche and are as deafening as a howling wind. They are condemning screams from tortured spirits that call you by name and attempt to drag you into their attacking rage. My temptation was to entertain the lies until their thoughts became mine. They were enticing me to stay in their god-forsaken grave and find some kind of twisted comfort in rehearsing the painful memories until self-pity and hatred could decompose my brain.

So this was it! This labyrinth of decay! Being a pastor's wife, I spent hours praying with others who were trying to make sense of their own horrifying nightmares. I listened as they asked the hard questions and supported them as they wrestled with their own doubts in the face of injustice and tragedy. I felt their sorrow and cried with them. But I had no idea, not until now, what this putrid pit was really like. However, I did know what it meant to never leave this place.

The refusal to let go of pain and not move on has catastrophic consequences. Clinging to the past hurts most assuredly guarantees a future without the possibility of healing both internally and relationally. Life can often become one sad story after another as we continue to just survive, chewing on the caustic roots of resentment and drinking from the stagnant pool of unforgiveness. The wounds from yesterday begin to fester and poison us. It is possible to willingly remain the victim and dwell forever in the gloomy dungeon of our past. Every lie that we believe as "truth" has the potential to bind us. Our agreement with deception erects a new wall, a self-made fortress, a useless attempt to protect ourselves from ever being hurt again.

This could happen to me! Just thinking those words almost took me to the ground. "God, where are you? Help me!" I had no answers for this beastly demon that was screeching in my head. At that moment I wasn't sure of anything. Was there a good God? Where was His protection? I was consumed with the feeling of abandonment.

There was nothing right about what had happened. Husbands are not supposed to betray their wives. Especially a Christian counselor! A missionary! The intensity of torment that was ripping at my soul was beyond anything I had ever experienced. Every scene replayed again and again in my mind. I think the worst part was the shame and the embarrassment that came with his action. We were supposed to be missionaries. Our venture overseas came to a screeching halt. We returned home completely shattered!

Staring through the dreary abyss, the stone-cold eyes of despair and hopelessness watched and waited. The moment I entertained the idea that there was no God, the two twisting vipers uncoiled and moved closer. Their hollow fangs dripped with venomous, hateful doubt and bitter unbelief. Stretching and hissing they strained to see if I would yield my will and agree to give up. Their poison was lethal. They wanted to inhabit my mind, and feed on my emotional pain.

This hellish horde was out to destroy my faith and rob my confidence in the compassion and goodness of my Creator which was the bedrock of my whole existence. To swallow their lies would mean my love would grow cold. In essence, my thoughts and eventually my emotions would agree to their terms. To bow would be the kiss of death!

Then something very profound happened. I remembered! It started with one thought. "We have a history together." For a split second, the whirling confusion in my mind stopped. I had never seen an angel. I'd never heard the audible voice of God. I'd never witnessed miraculous healing, and quite frankly, I didn't even have an inspiring conversion story. Still, somewhere from my inception there had always been... GOD! What I had was a lifetime of ordinary days that unmistakably and mysteriously were caressed by the Loving Hands of the Divine.

My mom's faith was my faith. She quietly lived it. She loved Jesus, and she taught me to love Him. Her faith was tangible because her character was consistent, and her love was reliable. Because of Mom, my relationship with my Heavenly Family was as real to me as my physical family. They were not some unapproachable phantom spirits, nor could They ever be reduced to a stale lifeless philosophy up for debate. They were as much a part of my history as Mom was. And I certainly did not need to defend

Their honor, especially to these wretched accusers! To deny Their existence altogether or worse, to blame Them for my husband's actions was unthinkable and even more unbearable than the grief that drove me to the street that day.

Ray of Hope

I made a decision to trust—to trust in Relationship, to trust Father, Son and Holy Spirit! Whom I could not see and could not feel! I chose God! And the moment I did, strength and courage took hold of me. Grace lifted my frail body and I stood. I whirled around to face the darkness, clenched my fists and hoarsely shrieked, "I don't understand any of this, but there is nothing wrong with God!"

As I wiped the warm tears off of my freezing cheeks, I turned a corner and came to a sudden stop. In the snow in front of me, a small purple crocus had pushed with all of its might through the frozen ground, and the heavy mantle of snow to be the first to trumpet the call of Spring and I heard the sweet voice of God.

"You have got to hang on, Debbie! Winter is almost over!"

I stood staring at this delightful ray of hope, basking in the warmth of my Comforter's voice. He assured me that just like this crocus had been given the fortitude to emerge through its darkness, so would I. I would face divorce and raise my children alone. There would be many other very cold and lonely winters, but never again would I be tempted to abandon my faith.

I purposely wrote this story personifying evil, because this unseen, devilish wickedness exists, and Satan's consuming hatred and intent to destroy is deeply personal! If you have experienced betrayal, especially from a spouse, you will understand. It can feel like a piece of us dies during the winter of a betrayal. Sorting through the debris, there are days that we wonder if we'll ever heal. We long for answers, honestly seeking understanding. It's important to finally stop asking why and begin to relax into the assurance that the real comfort we need will not come from explanations. Help will be realized through Relationship, Intimate Connection fortified within the realm of our spirit. The healing balm is being understood. Pain never subsides in the presence of answers. The only thing that will ultimately absorb the heartache is living in the Presence of Love, Incarnate, Powerful, Soothing, Presence! God's Presence and the presence of family and friends who are an extension of His compassionate heart and tender touch!

Dawn of a Heavenly Spring

Answers have come with time but only because my questions have changed. Or maybe I have changed. I underestimated the importance of my own faith-based history. I didn't grasp the gravity of Mom's dedication to the simple reading of Bible verses, nor was I aware of when my story had become part of God's larger story. I misjudged the devastation that is caused by sin, not just others' but my own and the reality of its source. I also undervalued the hidden blessing of trials which are inevitable and over the years have become the rebar supporting the foundation of my character. Calamity comes. People sometimes stumble and fall. And when they do, there are consequences, some greater and more painful than others. Right is right and wrong is wrong, and it is possible to know the difference. To be human is a wonder to behold. We are capable of performing the most glorious, selfless, heroic acts, but at the same time, we ALL are susceptible to both error and deception and cruelty. This has been true from the moment that mankind chose to believe the deceiver rather than God.

The disappointments do not have to leave us in despair but dependent—not on man but on the Son of Man who also suffered and was betrayed. Because of Him, there are endless possibilities for healing and wholeness. I know my Creator, Who has revealed and proven Himself over a lifetime to be a compassionate Father. He promised life and I believe Him. I really can look forward to the dawn of a heavenly Spring!

Leaning In:

- Where in your story have you experienced an attack on your faith?
- What did it reveal about who you are?
- What were the lies the enemy used to undermine your faith?
- Where do you run for comfort?

This is the life-giving message we heard him share and it's still ringing in our ears. We now repeat his words to you: God is pure light. You will never find even a trace of darkness in him.
(1 John 1:5, TPT)

Lord, I passionately love you and I'm bonded to you, for now you've become my power! You're as real to me as bedrock beneath my feet, like a castle on a cliff, my forever firm fortress, my mountain of hiding, my pathway of escape, my tower of rescue where none can reach me. My secret strength and shield around me, you are salvation's ray of brightness shining on the hillside, always the champion of my cause.
(Psalms 18:1-2, TPT)

8

CLOSE CALL ON THE I-5

PARENTING 101

It was in the fall of 1992, and I was not only recovering from the death of my marriage, I was also facing the reality of being a single mother, raising my two teenagers alone. It was the day after Thanksgiving Day, and my daughter and I were on our way to Centralia, WA to pick up her best friend. I was cruising down the I-5 in heavy traffic, engulfed in a torrential rainstorm. We were five minutes from our destination and for a split second, I took my eyes off of the road and glanced at Jamie. Returning my gaze, she gasped as our small Geo Storm veered to the left towards the car passing us. Without thinking, I jerked the steering wheel to the right and found myself in a hydroplane, totally out of control! Every attempt to regain contact with the wet asphalt failed. Our car smashed into the metal guard rail on the right and began to spin like the teacup ride at Disneyland. Miraculously, we didn't hit any other cars and our Geo finally came to a screeching halt as we collided into the center divider, now facing the on-coming cars.

My shaking fingers turned the key in an attempt to restart the engine. The front bumper looked like a crumpled newspaper and was jammed against what was left of our flat right tire. To the shrill sound of metal hitting metal, we managed to limp off of the freeway and onto the side of the road just as the next tidal wave of traffic passed. A very kind man who witnessed our devastating spin across the freeway stopped and gave us a ride into town where we met our friends. We made the necessary calls for help quickly, and then I headed back to my crushed little Storm to await the tow truck.

Alone and drenched, I closed my eyes and whispered to myself, "Deep breath. You're ok. Just breathe." My mind began to rewind the whole scene, replaying it in slow motion. I could still hear the sound of metal crunching, and each time my body would react with a shutter. "We could have been killed! You saved our lives. Thank you, Father!"

"*What happened?*" He asked. (I love this about our Father. Of course, He knew the answer. He just delights in engaging us in conversation.)

"I was going too fast. Jamie's response scared me, and I overreacted in fear. If I hadn't pulled the steering wheel so hard, we would have been fine."

"*That's right. Now, I want you to remember something.*"

"Ok, I'm listening." I sighed.

"*When you are raising teenagers, they will continually be overcome with emotion. Life will sometimes feel like a high-speed endless melodrama. The worst thing you can do as a mother is to overreact to their overreaction.*"

"Seriously, God?! A tip on parenting? You want to talk about this now?"

"*Yes! This is important! Overreactions will cause you to skid into a 'hydroplane' in your relationship with them every time, leaving you all damaged and in pain. Remember, a gentle, calm presence is what they need for stability and security.*"

I know it sounds crazy. But it's true. Talk about a teachable impacting moment! The memory of that day and the application of His wisdom and warning was profound and left a lasting impression, not only on my car but on my heart as well.

Lessons Learned

My world changed forever with the birth of my first child. In many ways, my kids and I were growing up together. My children were mirrors to my soul. In their child-like honesty, they were the ones who saw me at my worst and continually confronted my hypocrisy. "Do as I say, not as I do!" didn't cut it with my two. My only recourse was to change, and so Jesus continually used motherhood as an instrument of sanctification in my own personal growth. As a mom, I was forced to my knees on a daily basis, and dependence on the Holy Counselor became a way of life to help me raise my two very strong-willed children.

I remember when my daughter was two days old. She was so beautiful, all seven pounds of her, and I was dressing her in the hospital for the trip home. I held up her little undershirt for a moment, looked her in the eye and asked, "How am I going to get this thing on you?" My first attempt at squeezing her precious head through the microscopic hole in that fabric scared us both. She began to scream, which was the first of many "battles of the will" to come. Trembling with insecurity, I kissed her cheek and whispered, "Give me a break! I've never done this before."

That line could easily characterize our next eighteen years together. It doesn't matter how educated we are, how much practice we have had babysitting, or how many books we have read on child-rearing. It will never be enough. We don't get to choose our own temperament, and we absolutely have no say in the final configuration of our children's DNA either. Nor do they come with an owner's manual.

By the time my second child was born, my daughter was two

and I had learned volumes. At least I had the bathing and dressing thing down. We were thrilled to be blessed with a son. But once again, the life that I had known would never be the same.

As our family grew and the new personality was introduced to the mix, each member of our clan had to adjust. Every stage of development produced new dynamics and changes which only strengthened my resolve to ask for help. My constant prayer in raising my kids was simple and anything but profound. "What do I do now?" was constantly echoing throughout heaven. This was especially true as my two entered junior high school.

I found that adolescence was a metamorphic time in my kids' lives. Everything about them was changing, and just like emerging cocooned butterflies, they were extremely vulnerable, needing a bit of room to squirm and time for their developing independent wings to dry out.

My mothering instincts are strong, and everything inside me desperately wants to protect my children from harm. When they were babies and very young, this was an appropriate response. But as they grew older, my mothering style had to change. Training them to be leaders at times meant, respectfully backing off. There came a time when they had to learn to think for themselves, to be responsible and fly... without me!

Mothering Tightrope

When my son was ten years old, he began to learn Karate. As his mother, it was extremely difficult watching him on the mat with another boy being kicked around. I wanted to run and pick him up, and in some cases, the mother bear in me wanted to maul his opponent. But I knew that I had to stay on the bleacher. If I had entered that ring, Jason would have been humiliated beyond words. My place and my job was to cheer him on from the sidelines.

My teenagers needed encouragement during these transforming years more than ever before. We all felt a bit awkward. The three of us walked the parental-adolescent tightrope together. There were some intense moments. All of us messed up at times, but for the most part, these years were filled with fun and laughter. Mutual respect was always expected, and when we blew it, all of us just made a habit of asking for forgiveness.

There are times when I am overcome by the depth of joy that has been mine as a mother. To carry life, to participate in the birth of my two children, to love and nurture and to help them grow into the man and woman they are today has been the most demanding and yet rewarding endeavor of my life.

Parenting is hard work! But I think it is important to remember that growing up in this day and age is also excruciating and has become way more complicated over the years. So how do we not overreact when our children are transitioning out of childhood into young men and women and they are inappropriately spreading their wings? I believe that disrespectful behavior should always be addressed early on in our kids' lives. To provide consistent Godly instruction and loving discipline provides a child with security.

Fortunately, there are many great parenting resources available to come to our aid. For me, just knowing that the teen years would be an emotional rollercoaster helped immensely! But truly, I think our saving grace was having some quality families who lived life with us. When my kids couldn't hear from me but still needed an adult voice, there were other moms and dads who could speak truth and encourage them because we were connected and living in community. We were all in the thick of it together, and we all believed that "it takes a village to raise a child." We also believed that both adults and children were responsible for their own hearts and that every one of us is in need of loving-kindness, gentleness, a ton of mercy and forgiveness! Age makes no difference—adults or children—we are all kids of the King, and we are growing and learning together.

Another really unique attribute of our community was that we sincerely believed in our kids and saw them as unique and extremely valuable, no matter what their age. We taught them to hear from the Lord on their own, and they were encouraged to learn to serve and exercise their God-given gifts. We were exploring Kingdom life together.

As God has fathered us, I think we all were surprised at how He responded with compassion and understanding at the very moment that we were in the depths of a miserable failure. His confidence in us empowered our spirits to reach higher and be more. Over time, some of us have also come to appreciate His discipline, as we have been forced to walk out the consequences of our bad choices. He is the perfect model of a parent!

Love covers all things—that is kindness and mercy. Love bears all things—that is selfless, patient nurturing. Love hopes all things —that is endless encouragement. Love never ends—that is unconditional forgiveness and acceptance, bringing growth and life. That is being a parent!

Leaning In:

- What is your parenting or mentoring experience teaching you about yourself?
- How might your strategy need to change?
- What is one small step that you could take to grow in your parenting or leadership skills?
- What does your community support system look like? If it is lacking, who can you reach out to create one?

Fathers, don't exasperate your children, but raise them up with loving discipline and counsel that brings the revelation of our Lord.
(*Ephesians* 6:4, TPT)

If you refuse to discipline your children, it proves you don't love them; if you love your children, you will be prompt to discipline them.
(*Proverbs* 13:24, TLB)

Teach a child to Choose the right path, and when they are older, he will remain upon it.
(*Proverbs* 22:6, TLB)

9

BACK TO SCHOOL AT FORTY

HIGHER EDUCATION

Have you ever had an idea that seems utterly ridiculous, unreachable, and absolutely impossible? And somewhere in your heart, there is a nagging suspicion that it might be God's idea, that He was just waiting for you to think it and then ask for it? This is where the seed of His faith is planted deep within our desires. Depending on the condition of the soil in our heart, and whether we take the necessary steps to care for it, the sprout will either wither in unbelief or it can grow into our very own Pharaoh-fighting, Egypt-exiting, Red Sea-rending miracle story! This was MY dream story!

Here I was sitting in class at one of the most prominent universities in the country. I had been away from Pepperdine for twenty-three years. That's a long time to be away from the academic world. My education was the only thing in my life that I had not completed. In 1974, instead of finishing my degree in religion, I chose to marry the most promising student within the department. I left school, married and two years later we started our family. My education continued outside the classroom.

Being allowed to return to Malibu, California and complete

my degree was absolutely one of the greatest gifts and miracles of my entire life. My professor was a pretty blond with light blue eyes. Had she not been standing in front of the class handing out my syllabus, I never would have guessed that she was our instructor.

She looked young enough to be one of the students in this class. As I watched her, I immediately felt that we had something in common. We were both nervous! This was her first day teaching Statistics at this very prestigious university and my first day of school. I was a returning student, a second semester junior and old enough to be her mother.

My professor began with a basic review of algebra. Did I even have algebra in high school? I couldn't remember. Panic hit like an unexpected wave of the ocean. I held my breath as the undertow of fear began sucking me into its swift current of doubt, tearing at my confidence. What was I thinking? My mind began to swell with one suffocating thought after another.

"I am no student! I'm not smart enough to be here! I didn't do well 23 years ago. What makes me think I can do any better now? I hate math! I hated it in high school, and I can't do it now. I am going to fail! I can't believe I asked God for this!"

In one second, all of my hopes and the thrill of watching my Provider perform miracle after miracle had vanished. All I could hear was the blaring battle cry of my hateful enemy, insecurity, boasting of my imminent doom. I was no different than the children of Israel being delivered from Egypt. In a single breath, those elated emancipated slaves forgot the powerful deliverance story and became recoiling cowards at the first sight of Pharaoh's fallout!

After class, I ran to the truck, my familiar sanctuary. For me, this Ford was like the hand of Jesus, tenderly catching every tear and faithfully hiding me as I allowed myself to be real. Here I could safely process, feeling the immense span of emotions that I now understand to be part of my God-breathed personality experiencing the abundant life that He promised. Whether it was a day full of joyful singing, smiles and giggles or a moment to draw from the seemingly bottomless well of my past stuffed emotions, this was a holy place. It was the first new automobile I had ever purchased, thanks to my dad, and it represented a new beginning, the rebuilding of my life.

My fingers gripped the steering wheel as my father's face and an encouraging smile appeared in my mind. He was my hero. His hands were as tough as a worn piece of leather, which was a perfect portrayal of his life. What a character! Benny Alls was a hard-working trucker with a dream in his heart to build boats. One day at age forty, instead of dumping another load of asphalt, he dumped his Mack truck, and he and my brother began Metalcraft Marine. They have been building boats ever since.

My father was not afraid to take a risk, and I was banking on the fact that the Alls' grit was written somewhere within my own DNA. One thing I knew for certain. The Almighty's Faith had moved every mountain between Washington and California to get us here. It happened so quickly and against such incredible odds. Only God could have pulled this off!

Just a few months ago, I had been bent over, furiously scrubbing the last filthy Jacuzzi tub of the day. It was huge, and so wide that I had to crawl into the center of the scummy thing to reach the far corner. Soft Scrub wasn't cutting it! My vision began to blur. Was that sweat or tears? Frustration consumed me. I was so thankful that the owner of this cesspool wasn't home.

I sat back on my heels and cried, "Lord, there has got to be more to my life than this."

Stepping Out

It was Dad's idea to start my own cleaning business, which turned out to be quite successful. After the divorce, the kids and

I lived in a 26-foot trailer on his land overlooking the Puget Sound. Between the nurturing love of my parents and the pristine rugged beauty of the Northwest, we were on the mend. For a while, we were forced to seek financial aid from social services, which for me was almost as devastating as having my marriage fail. But within just a few months, I was able to make enough to pay our monthly bills, freeing us from our dependence on welfare.

The greatest blessing of being self-employed was the flexibility in my schedule which allowed me to continue homeschooling my children. They were my top priority, the joy of my life, and I was determined to do whatever it took to salvage what was left of our little family.

In response to my prayer that day in the bathroom, the conversation in my mind went something like this:

God asked, "*What would you like to do?*"

Without hesitation, I answered, "I want to go back to college. I want to finish what I started. Maybe if I had more training, I could help these difficult teenagers that You keep drawing into my life. But I don't want to go to school in Washington. What I really want is to go back to Pepperdine and finish my degree there in California."

He cheerfully replied, "*OK, let's do that!*"

I booked a ticket, flew to California and met with some dear friends who were classmates from the '70s and were now employed at Pepperdine. They encouraged me to meet with the Dean of Admission, who "coincidentally" was also a friend from college. I had no idea that he worked at Pepperdine. I told him my story and of my desire to finish my degree. He listened intently and then said, "Let me see what I can do."

He went before the Admissions Board and was given permission to re-enroll me under my old catalog of 1972. This allowed the transference of all of my previous credits. We discussed the requirements of their decision and then he asked, "Don't you have a daughter who is about to graduate from high school?"

I said, "Yes. I have been home-schooling her. She is almost finished with her junior year."

Then he sat forward in his chair and asked, "Do you think she could finish her junior and senior year by next summer? If so, we could enroll her in our Summer Bridge program. She could start in the summer, and you could join her in the fall."

The shock left my mind reeling. What if I had not come? What if I had dismissed the notion of pursuing this dream? I had no way of knowing what the future held, and I certainly had no clue that this decision would also be preparing the way for my daughter. Only God! From welfare to Pepperdine! We still had no money. Not for this. The financial aid officer gave us both everything that was available—grants, scholarships, and student loans. Water from a rock! Manna from heaven! (By the way, unbeknownst to me, this move also set in motion a plan that would place my son in the right place at the right time to launch his music career. One year after I graduated, he would sign with DreamWorks and his band, Lifehouse, would rise to the top of the charts.)

There are times when our Deliverer demands that you remove the slave band from your neck and follow His lead. And it is not uncommon for Him to give you a personal tour through the wilderness of your heart on the way to your "promise land." For us hard-headed types, He will take us right over the banks of our solid human reasoning and urge us to walk with Him through a sea of logic-defying circumstances. On this hike, it is not wise to linger and marvel at the towering waterworks during your miraculous escape. It's smart to run as fast as you can until you reach the other side of the deliverance. If you wait around and try to figure out the how's and why's of God, you will miss the show! (If you want a fabulous read, check out the book of Exodus in the Bible.)

This Was My Story!

I glanced down at my knuckles, now white from gripping the steering wheel. Instead of releasing my grip, I clenched my teeth and bore down even harder. With eyes closed, I wrestled the slimy insecurity and began to put the squeeze on doubt. I rehearsed every detail of the Almighty's miraculous intervention. Faith began to strangle the unbelief in my heart. My words sliced through the heaviness that hung in the air.

I was not Moses! I had no wonder rod to swallow up my slithering enemies. But I recognized that what I did have was much more powerful. I had God, Himself, claiming me as His daughter and His power had moved heaven and earth to allow me to have my heart's desire.

Whether it's an Egyptian army taking a dive and becoming the new dazzling décor of the deep or my very own personal giant of insecurity being skinned, deboned and filleted, it is still deliverance. It is absolutely supernatural, no big deal for my Defender, and a whole lot of freedom for me.

In order to retrain my brain and help me to thrive in the academic wilderness that stretched before me, Wisdom gave me a very interesting strategy. I was to park in the lowest parking lot by the gym and walk to class every day climbing a set of stairs that at first felt like an assent to Mt Sinai. Later it became more like walking the "Green Mile"!

If you have ever lived in Malibu, you know that the hills rule. Any construction and all landscape must conform to their strict demands and add to the original glorious design. The Pepperdine campus is perched on the lap of this magnificent terrain and bows to the majesty of the sun, rolling hills and the glorious Pacific Ocean. Needless to say, parking is always an adventure. And every student gets an aerobic workout whether they want it or not.

My program was not just about physical fitness or the exercising of my mind. I had a Personal Trainer who was more interested in the "buffness" of my soul. He was ruthless with each lie that held me down. And quite frankly, my Coach didn't care if I came to class looking like I had just crawled away from a wrestling match. This time I was not at Pepperdine to receive a "MRS. Degree." It was not about looking cute or boys. These were my instructions:

"As you climb each step, I want you to repeat these words. 'Every time I read a book, I will comprehend and remember more. Each test I take will become easier and easier. I can do this. I can learn.'"

Every day for the next year and a half, those words became my personal cheering section, calming me and keeping the anxiety of endless projects, tests and grades at bay. I worked and God blessed it. I was focused and He empowered me. I studied into the wee hours of the morning and He sustained me. I never did overcome being nervous when taking a test or giving an oral report. But we did it. I graduated with honors and pulled straight A's!

As for the Statistics class, at the end of the trimester my professor came to me and said, "Deb, you have consistently had the highest scores of any student in your class. If you will help me tutor some of your struggling classmates, you will be exempt from having to take the final exam."

I still hate math. But the fear of failure is dying. The fact that I even passed is mind-boggling. That I was asked to help teach it is even more bewildering.

Permission to Ask

Pepperdine is where my adult life began. I had come full circle. Thanks to my Heavenly Father and dear friends I had been given another chance, more than a chance! This was more like winning the lottery or being given a Disneyland's FastPass ticket to bypass the crowds of brilliant scholars, eagerly waiting in line for Mr. Toad's wild ride in "Academia Land"! This time I finished. So did my daughter. Unlike her mother though, it didn't take her forty years to learn the lessons!

So what is lying around in the deep dark cavern of your desires? You have permission to bring it out in the open. Jesus is the one inviting, "*Ask me. What do you want?*"

One of the most precious moments that I experienced on this trek was the scummy bathtub encounter. I love having the freedom to just be me, to be real with the Lord. He is so refreshing. He listens. He asks questions. And He is honestly interested in me. It is really difficult for some of us to wrap our heads around the reality that Jesus is really eager to hear the details of our desires and hopes and dreams. And He is asking, "*What would you like to do?*"

Dreaming is part of our God-Image. We have been destined to be co-creators, despite our age, despite our circumstances. I have never met a child who could not create. Their ability to use their imagination is absolutely inspiring. We adults, on the other hand, especially those who have been kicked around by life's onslaught of discouragement, can shut down. So many of us have experienced so much disappointment in our lives that we quit dreaming. We are afraid to hope and don't want to experience the crushing blow of another failure. We just give up. And in that painful place, there is a loving Father who desires to come close. He knows us and has seen us hurting and understands our fear and reluctance to venture out again. But He also knows what we are missing, what could be right around the corner.

One of the most fascinating truths about the ways of God is His brilliant timing. He does His deepest work on our character in the waiting—sometimes a lifetime of waiting for our deepest unfulfilled desires to manifest. His timing is one of the greatest mysteries to us kids who are trapped within our own locked-in thinking. It's easy to understand why. We have been created within the constraints of time which can make us a bit impatient, and we lack the infinite perspective of the Master Planner.

Abraham is one of my favorite Biblical mentors. His story chronicles his journey of desire to be a father. He was desperate to have a son, which was foretold, but God's plan was much bigger than even for him to be a *father of nations*. His relational roots grew deep, pushing through the dark, hard soil of unfulfilled longing which gave birth to his life "being call." It was Abraham's decision to walk with God DURING the decades of his tarrying dream, which transformed his being into the "*father of our faith*"! Perhaps it was the process of waiting in the promise, (imperfectly, I might add), that prepared him to display the prophetic Heart of God. When tested, his faith rose to obedience, even being willing to sacrifice his one and only son, *even though God had told him, "Isaac is the son through whom your descendants will be counted." Abraham reasoned that if Isaac died, God was able to bring him back to life again. And in a sense, Abraham did receive his son back from the dead.* (Hebrews 11: 18-19, NLT)

I wonder if this test and his response was the reason he was born. I wonder if this was the pinnacle of his life call. I doubt that Abraham had a clue about the importance of this moment. How could he possibly know that at the very instant he lifted the knife to sacrifice his son, his faith would prophetically display the sacrificial Heart of God and His Son? His trust in the goodness of God had obviously been passed on to Isaac, his promised child. Both of their courageous obedience opened the heavenly curtains for a sneak preview into the piercing plan that was set in motion from the moment sin was conceived in the garden. Abraham's dream for a son was no different than God's dream. From the very beginning, Yahweh's desire was to draw mankind to Himself, to be Father.

There are so many nuggets that we can gather from this story. We just can't know the full scope of God's dream for us. Some of us get bits and pieces, which are given in a timely manner, but I find that the incomplete picture of His dream which is growing in my heart promotes a very necessary dependence on Him.

What are the clues you are discovering as you search your heart? Abraham's journey was initiated by God coming and speaking a promise over his life. He was invited to leave all that he knew and go after the promise. What has God spoken over you? What is the idea that is rolling around in your heart that seems unreachable? It is only unreachable if you stay where you are. If you are being prompted *to go*, don't let fear stop you. The invitation comes from a gentle Shepherd who will lead and protect you all the way. Walk with Him in the waiting. Who knows where your faith will lift you?

Leaning In:

- If you had all the resources that you needed and knew that you could not fail, what would you want to do?
- What is God revealing about you in the waiting?
- What if all the circumstances in your life right now were aligning themselves to launch your faith to a new level of breakthrough? What act of obedience might release that?
- What is the promise that the Father has spoken over you?

After his soul becomes a guilt-offering, he will gaze upon his many offspring and prolong his days. And through him, Yahweh's deepest desires will be fully accomplished. After the great anguish of his soul, he will see light and be fully satisfied. By knowing him, the righteous one, my servant will make many to be righteous, because he, their sin-bearer, carried away their sins.

(*Isaiah* 53:10-11, *TPT*)

10

A PIONEER SPIRIT

WHEN THE GOING GETS TOUGH

I wonder why God chose 1954 as the year of my birth. So many times, I have thought that I should have been born in my great-grandmother's era. I am a pioneer woman. The greater the challenge, the more determined I become to overcome whatever obstacles are in my way. I can just see myself wearing my homemade dress and bonnet sitting in a covered wagon headed west.

Well... maybe not! Now that I think this through, perhaps the good Lord, in His infinite wisdom, created me in just the right year. The fact is, it doesn't matter what era we live in. The world will always need people with pioneer spirits because He will never stop creating. Our loving Father is always looking for adventurous children to help him birth new things.

Three years after graduating from Pepperdine, I left the security of a very well-paying job, including an office with an ocean view, my home, my family and friends in California, and drove north to help establish a new ministry in Port Townsend, Washington. Youth With a Mission (YWAM) had been given the opportunity to establish a training center on a nine-acre camp across the street from Discovery Bay. The location was beautiful, but the buildings were in great need of repair. The camp belonged to a local, extremely conservative church foundation, and we were being allowed to use the facility rent-free in exchange for our services to upgrade and maintain it.

I arrived as the first "'YWAMer" and became the administrator of the camp. I moved into the caretaker's home in July and had one month to get the buildings ready for our first incoming camp in August.

The first day that I drove up to look at the property is etched in my mind. I parked across the street and sat there in a daze. As my eyes scanned each acre and the detail of every building, I was completely overwhelmed by the immensity of the job before me. It would take an army to pull this off. It seemed insurmountable!

I got out of my truck and stood at the front of the property and for a moment turned my back on the camp. Directly across the street was a panoramic view of the Olympic Mountains framing the splendor of Discovery Bay. Chills ran down my arm as a Psalm of David burst from the depths of my spirit: *I look up to the mountains and hills, longing for God's help. But then I realize that our true help and protection come only from the Lord, our Creator who made the heavens and the earth.* (Psalm 121:1, TPT)

Taking a deep breath, I turned back to the "impossible" and in my heart began to create. I envisioned a new lodge built where I was standing, and the old buildings refurbished and painted. I could see green lawns and beautiful flower gardens surrounding each building. Walking paths through the woods could be created with scattered benches for resting, and a covered gazebo with climbing roses. My imagination went wild as excitement and joy began to fill my cup. The words of an old Sunday School song began to replay in my heart: "Nothing is impossible with Him." As the words danced around my mind, I began to pray that God would send me helpers and that what I was seeing in my spirit would someday materialize.

There is a certain amount of adrenaline and natural momentum that comes with a new challenge. It is an adventure, and most people start off strong and do well. But it is when the newness of the journey wears off, we get weary, or when unexpected challenges begin to mount that our zeal and energy can wane.

In the beginning, I felt like Wonder Woman. I started scrubbing and painting, gardening and networking within the community. Soon we had a small team of volunteers, and within a month, the little camp seemed to come alive. One of my responsibilities included being a liaison between YWAM and our new partners of the foundation. To my dismay, I discovered a faction existed amongst the board members and the marriage between our two ministries was not unanimously accepted. Unfortunately, I was the face of YWAM, the only one living at the camp, and I was about to "enter the ring" with a handful of the local, resistant remnants, led by one very angry, domineering matriarch.

The attacks that catch me off-guard and undo me the most are the ones that show up from those who are supposed to be on my own team. Every day I poured my energy into every square inch of a piece of land that didn't even belong to me. I wanted everything to be clean and beautiful for the foundation as their first camp was coming in August. But I was also thoroughly enjoying working with my friends to build a future site for our YWAM schools. In my innocence, I just assumed that everyone would be as thrilled with the progress as I was.

Unexpected Opposition

One day I walked into the kitchen behind the dining hall and was surprised to meet one of our neighboring board members and his wife. She and I had never met, so I excitedly introduced myself. The moment her eyes fixed on mine, I literally found myself stepping back. It felt as if I was in the presence of a raging cat that was ready to pounce on me and rip me to shreds! Shocked by her angry demeanor and the apologetic awkwardness of her husband, I abruptly ended the encounter with, "Well, it was nice to meet you.", which in this case was blatantly a lie. I made a break for the back exit and sprinted home.

Back at the trailer, I shut the door and quickly locked it just in case I had been followed. My heart was racing as I relived the scene. "What was that?" I whispered. This was a first for me. Never before had I experienced such an aggressive and unkind greeting, especially from a pastor's wife.

I was unfamiliar with the culture and practices of this particular religious breed. Not long after that unpleasant exchange in the kitchen, I found myself once again face to face, this time with her husband. I had just completed a two-day project painting the interior walls of the meeting hall which the owners called the "tabernacle." In the front of the room was an old stage with a piece of railing bolted to the center edge of the platform, constructed out of old 2"x 4" pieces of lumber. I had a bit of paint left from the walls, so I slapped it on the wood as my final finishing touch. As I started to clean up, I heard the door open and turned to see the man walking toward me. I gave him a warm welcome and then cheerfully asked, "What do you think?"

His eyes widened, his jaw dropped, and he gasped in a hushed whimper, "You painted the altar?!"

"Uh, yeah. It needed it! You're kidding me, right?" I nervously laughed.

His expression didn't change, and he looked at me with unrelenting, piercing eyes. I called him by name and said, "Oh no. I had no idea. I am so sorry! I will strip it off as soon as it dries."

He hung his head and said, "Never mind, just leave it." Then he slowly turned and made his way out the door just as my wobbly knees buckled. I reached for the stage to steady my balance and then sat down in the silence, one hand covering my mouth to smother a cry, the other on my stomach as if a touch would somehow keep me from throwing up. I looked at the wood altar now gleaming with fresh paint. How could I have known that those 2x4s were sacred? I had no history, no grid for understanding altar protocol. This was an innocent mistake. It was done. And for the moment, so was I. I was wrecked!

Cat Fight

Each of the following days began with a long "To Do" list. My team and I worked from dawn to dusk. As we addressed the plumbing and water lines of this facility, I was forced to seek assistance from an old-timer and his wife who lived a few miles away. They were one of the founding families of the camp and had the same cold and unfriendly attitude as the pastor's wife. This time I was more prepared for the initial meeting. With quiet resolve, I continually responded to them with respect and a cheerful heart. Over time they seem to soften a bit. I could even get a giggle out of them once in a while.

Then the day of the first camp arrived. Their church staff were gathering in the tabernacle. I went in to make sure they had everything they needed, but before I could speak a word, the pastor's wife began to verbally accost me. Her hateful voice got louder and louder as she hurled accusations, and then she started coming closer as if she was going to punch me in the face. I glanced at the elderly couple whom I thought had become my friends. They all just stood there staring at me.

I held up my hand motioning for her to stop, and then calmly said, "I am not here to fight you. Everything we have done has been approved by your board." I turned and started to walk away.

She continued her ranting, following me out the door. I honestly expected to be tackled from behind and was envisioning a full-on "catfight." By the time I reached the door of my house, I was shaking all over. I quickly packed a bag and drove to a friend's home for the night. We cried together, but it wasn't long before we were both howling and laughing at the very thought of a pastor's wife and a missionary having a ladies wrestling match on the grass in front of their beloved tabernacle.

The following Monday, I woke up depressed and began scanning the classifieds for a new job. My eyes fell on an ad seeking an administrative assistant for a church in the next town. I called and set up an appointment for an interview. Within the first five minutes, I knew that I was not in the will of God. I couldn't focus, couldn't type, couldn't remember how to spell and basically failed all of their tests. The humiliation continued as I sat before the interview board answering their questions. Finally, I brought the time to a close. Explaining my situation and with an honest confession that I felt a little like Jonah running from God, I left.

I Am Not Leaving!

I returned to the camp hanging my head in shame. Before I was even able to apologize, I felt the Lord's embrace. In silence, we walked together towards the bay. Off in the distance, hugging the outer left corner of the tabernacle garden, was a blanket of purple. It immediately aroused my curiosity because I had never seen any flowers growing there before. Drawing closer, I dropped to my knees in astonishment and drew a small cluster of crocus gently into my hand.

"You planted crocus that bloom in the summer? Oh, thank you, Father!"

I began to laugh and cry at the same time. This was my flower of hope! Here I was again struggling to endure another season of disappointment and rejection. His affection and encouragement was being released from these upward-facing, cup-shaped beauties. He didn't seem at all concerned about my failure. In fact, it felt like He had ignored the entire episode. As we walked back to my home, I began to realize how close I had come to quitting. People were not my enemy. My attackers were not flesh and blood. Righteous anger arose within me, and I asked, "I am only one little woman and the enemy is trying to drive me out. What can I do to fight back?"

The Lord responded, *"Paint your mobile home. It is an act of faith that speaks a loud message, 'I am NOT leaving!'"*

What a brilliant battle strategy! I immediately went and purchased the paint, and with every stroke of the brush and roll of the roller, I drove our stake into the spiritual ground of that land. As I dug in my heels, refusing to leave, I rolled up my sleeves and our team led an army of volunteers sent by the Most High to completely renovate the entire facility. Some of what I envisioned that first day has come true. Some are still to come. Today the camp has been gifted to Youth With a Mission, and it has become another successful training facility, sending students across the globe to fulfill the great commission.

A Pioneer Spirit

Following God and being in His will brings a joy and contentment that far surpasses the challenges which will always accompany any pioneering venture. There is nothing more fulfilling than to partner with the Master Designer and His people, working together to accomplish an "impossible" mission. And there is nothing more humbling than experiencing His gracious acceptance as He covers my weakness.

Out of all that the Holy Spirit taught me in those three years, the one thing that brought me the most freedom and comfort in the midst of that God-sized project was His word: "*I am not holding you responsible for the outcome of this, only the next thing that I tell you to do.*"

Now that is good news! As I think about this, I am aware that there has been an expansion in my thinking. Perhaps my definition of being a "pioneer" is being broadened and redefined. Whether I am building a home, launching a business or raising a child, a pioneering exploit is in play. Whether I am in a leadership position or part of a team supporting and serving someone else's vision, I am still pioneering.

The last commission of Jesus to go into the world and create disciples is a Kingdom Pioneering command and that is meant to be carried out within every realm of our existence. The "doing" role we play is not the point. It is the pioneering work within our "being", the heart of a pioneer, that is at stake.

It is about the development of our character. I am learning that it takes faithfulness to continually press in—to see, to catch the Heavenly Vision for your next step. It takes steadfastness and courage to push through the obstacles, and sometimes blatant attacks and not quit. Hunger and thirst for righteousness drive us to the well of Living Water to receive the refreshing relief needed to persevere and do the next right thing. The fruit of patience grows as we trust and rest in the reassurance that His burden is light. Our striving is unnecessary and unproductive. If we are to finish well in whatever pioneering venture we do, it is imperative that we recognize and partner with the building process and work being done within our hearts. Only then can we bring to our individual environments the true Spirit needed to create from scratch that which did not exist before. Our spirits can actually partner with the Holy Spirit to brood over whatever chaos exists and we can co-create order by speaking life. This is pioneering at its best! All of us are *Image-bearers*, which makes all of us potential pioneers.

Leaning In:

- What area in your heart is under construction in your pioneering venture?
- What small step can you take to partner with the Spirit's work in this area?
- What "doing" role have you been called to pioneer?
- What are some of the obstacles that stand in your way?
- As you lean in to hear your Heavenly Consultant, what is His strategy to overcome them?

Keep me safe, O mighty God. I run for dear life to you, my safe place. So I said to the Lord God, "You are my Maker, my Mediator, and my Master. Any good thing you find in me has come from you." And he said to me, "My holy lovers are wonderful, my majestic ones, my glorious ones, fulfilling all my desires." Yet there are those who yield to their weakness, and they will have troubles and sorrows unending. I never gather with such ones, nor give them honor in any way. Lord, I have chosen you alone as my inheritance. You are my prize, my pleasure, and my portion. I leave my destiny and its timing in your hands. Your pleasant path leads me to pleasant places. I'm overwhelmed by the privileges that come with following you, for you have given me the best. The way you counsel and correct me makes me praise you more, for your whispers in the night give me wisdom, showing me what to do next. Because you are close to me and always available, my confidence will never be shaken, for I experience your wrap-around presence every moment. My heart and soul explode with joy—full of glory! Even my body will rest confident and secure. For you will not abandon me to the realm of death, nor will you allow your Holy One to experience corruption. For you bring me a continual revelation of resurrection life, the path to the bliss that brings me face-to-face with you.

(Psalms 16, TPT)

11

DO YOU REALLY WANT A HAMBURGER?

DESIRE OR DRIVE-THROUGH?

The knock at my door that morning was an intrusion. I had to guard my time of quiet and reflection, sometimes having to rise way before the sun. Instinct told me that these moments were my life-line to sanity and the infusion of peace that would guard me throughout the rest of the day. I contemplated hiding and pretending that I didn't hear the knock. But finally, with a heavy sigh, I threw on my robe and went to greet my early guest. Her eyes were filled with tears, and the anguish on her face left me with a knot in my stomach. As she shared her story and her need to get to the airport, my mind began to race as this would mean a total disruption of my planned day. I got dressed, made some phone calls and off we went. The airport was two and a half hours away, and fortunately, because it was the weekend, we missed all the work traffic.

After dropping her off, I headed for the ferry in Seattle. As I pulled into the gate and saw the long line of cars awaiting the arrival of the next boat, my heart began to sink. I hadn't eaten anything all day. I was hungry and emotionally drained and just wanted to be at home. Turning off the engine of my truck, I remembered that there was a McDonald's restaurant close by, so I grabbed my purse and headed for the golden arches. It appeared that everyone else had the same idea. I approached the end of the line which at that point was outside the front door. My irritation began to increase with every step. As I waited, a very strange question interrupted my moodiness. *"Do you really want a hamburger?"*

I immediately recognized His voice, and as I pondered the question, I thought, "No. What I would love to have is a juicy steak."

"Then why are you in line at McDonald's?" His query created a jolt in my being like leaning up against a live electrical wire.

The truth was, I hadn't even considered what I really wanted. I was just attempting to relieve the uncomfortable empty feeling in my stomach. With visions of tender, seasoned morsels of a fillet grilled to perfection, a creamy baked potato, fresh delicate salad greens and homemade, hot bread, I headed back to the truck.

Finally, the ferry arrived. I started my engine and waited anxiously, but to my horror, the car in front of me was the last one they would allow on board. I was trapped! I couldn't get out of line and there was nothing I could do but wait another fifty minutes for the next boat. My irritation returned and with it, the growling from my complaining stomach intensified. Once again with my wallet in hand, I headed for McDonald's, only to find the line even longer than the first time.

He asked again, *"Do you really want a hamburger? Are you willing to wait for your heart's desire, or are you going to settle for a quick fix?"*

Something told me that this conversation was about much more than just a hamburger. Jesus' questions always have a purpose and this time the impact felt more like a bolt of lightning. As I walked back to the truck, I couldn't help but grin. I was His captive. He had my total attention for the next fifty minutes.

The wonderful thing about being single was the gift of time to do a lot of soul-searching. For ten years, I had grown in my understanding of myself and found an element of independence and contentment as I embraced the season. Even so, there was an honest longing to be a wife again, and I found myself being tested in a new relationship that had recently developed. He was handsome and fun, and there was incredible potential, but... something was missing. Our lives were not going in the same direction. We weren't passionate about the same things. He was filling an immediate need in my life. I liked the attention and companionship, but time was revealing what was in our hearts and the truth was, we were not on the same path.

In earnest reflection, I prayed all the way home and laid my desire for a husband at His feet. I knew what I had to do. Once again, I gave up my grid for what I thought I needed in a relationship and asked Him to guide me. I would wait.

When I arrived home, I drove to my favorite restaurant in Port Townsend and ordered the best steak on the menu. I had the perfect corner table overlooking the water. The moment was glorious. At last, my steak arrived. I took the first bite... and to my utter dismay, it wasn't at all as yummy as I had remembered. I sat back in my chair and could just see the Lord grinning at me.

"What is this? You did it again! Another setup!" I quietly moaned into my napkin.

"Someday when I give you your heart's desire, remember that your husband will never be your Savior; he will still be just a man. Sometimes it's possible that your high expectations are based on an imaginary illusion, and that will make reality a disappointment every time."

I don't think I will ever become accustomed to the mystery of the Spirit's involvement in my life. He continues to touch my heart at times when I least expect it. That is the miracle of His goodness that excites and feeds my spirit. It moves me deeply because I can sense His heart, which genuinely cares to know what is dear to me. My desires are important to Him and I am not only given permission to have them, but I know that He will provide the resolve to wait and discover HIS fulfillment, HIS way and in HIS time.

This was not the first time that He had challenged me to reach higher, nor would it be the last gentle correction redirecting my mind towards embracing truth. I feel like a child on tiptoe grasping for my Father's surprise treat as He daily leans into my personal space to offer only the best and the most satisfying tastes. As I chew on each tasty morsel of wisdom, I am finding that my appreciation for the same heavenly food that sustained Jesus as He walked the earth is growing and changing my earthly pallet of desire. I am beginning to experience His words: *My food is to be doing the will of him who sent me and bring it to completion.* (John 4:34, TPT)

It makes me wonder—what is on the menu? What is His work that I will need to finish?

Leaning In:

- What is the desire that might be hidden within your own heart?
- What might be your own "quick fix" solution to fill that desire?
- What would it look like for you to NOT settle?
- What is on the Chef's menu that has your name written on it?

May God give you every desire of your heart and carry out your every plan as you go to battle. When you succeed, we will celebrate

and shout for joy. Flags will fly when victory is yours! Yes, God will answer your prayers and we will praise him. I know God gives me all that I ask for and brings victory to his anointed king. My deliverance cry will be heard in his holy heaven. By his mighty hand miracles will manifest through his saving strength.
(*Psalms* 20:4-6, TPT)

12

BONSAI

PERFECTLY BOUND

My body shot up in bed, heart pounding and my mind reeling! It was just a dream. Taking a deep breath, I fell back onto my pillow as each scene replayed...

Get out your paper and number from 1-30.

The moment of terror! School had never been easy for me, not because I couldn't learn or that I wasn't smart enough. I was just so painfully shy and uncertain about myself. I was crippled by fear, bound by the cruel words from peers and siblings that shaped me as a child and continued to shackle me as an adult.

Today I felt more like the frightened little girl back in grammar school rather than a confident university student. Not only had I not prepared for this final, I had not even opened the textbook. How did I let this happen? My life had been so hectic that somehow in all of the craziness, I had neglected this class altogether. Now it was too late. I was sitting at the back of the room in a panic, trying to remember any shred of information from the lectures that might help. I did recall the professor saying that we would be tested on the Gospel of John. The Bible had always been an important part of my life. Maybe I could draw on that and pass at least part of this test. My thoughts were interrupted as he repeated the command again to get out our paper. My face felt hot and flushed as I frantically searched for a clean piece of paper. I couldn't find one unused sheet. With trembling hands, I began to erase a paragraph from a page and tried to steady my hand enough to print the numbers.

I glanced up just in time to see my professor walking over to a CD player. He hit a switch and the room filled with beautiful music. As I listened to the lyrics, I realized that it was a worship song, and the lyrics were full of clues to help us with the answers to the questions. "What a merciful teacher!" I thought to myself.

Then as the music continued, he picked up a potted plant from his desk and placed it on a table. Two mysterious young men, unknown to my classmates and me, approached the table. To the beat of the music, they began to pound on the plant. By this time we were all straining to see what they were doing. With each downbeat, I could hear the sound of a snap like wires breaking. Leaning closer, I caught a glimpse of the pot. It was a Bonsai tree. My professor picked up the tiny pot and walked straight to my desk and placed it into my hands. As I examined the miniature evergreen, I touched the limbs where the wires had cut into the bark. "It doesn't look perfect anymore, but it is free," I whispered.

Without saying a word, he took the tree back to his desk and picked up another plant. This time he came to me with a stunning sunflower. It was healthy and strong and had been allowed to grow in complete freedom. He placed it on my desk, looked deeply into my eyes, smiled and then walked away.

Now fully awake, I closed my eyes and saw the tiny Bonsai tree and then the sunflower. "What was that about?" I asked.

My mind began to race. Scenes from my life's journey began to flash across the screen of my mind. I began to hear dialogue from the past—spoken words, biting words, crippling words. Unrealistic expectations that others had placed on me and some of which I had placed on myself were gripping me and shaping me. Like the little Bonsai, I was stunted, and my soul was twisted and bent. I was bound by old, forgotten memories, moments where the hateful words attached themselves to me like the wires that cut into the tiny limbs of that tree. Thoughts about Sunday school and harsh religious teachers began to materialize before my eyes. It was like the scene in the Wizard of Oz, where Dorothy stands before the crystal ball crying out for Auntie Em, only to have the wicked witch show up with her frightful mocking.

Rigid religious law had been choking my life flow. That's what legalism does. Outwardly, you portray the illusion of perfection (at least seen through your own blinded eyes). Everything seems to be in its place. But in reality, every movement is labored and seems to be forced by some unseen task-master. The Bonsai tree was the perfect image of my past identity.

Preparation

The dream itself signified a new season that I entered. I moved to a new town, a new home, a new job, a new church, and new friends. It felt like I had entered my "promise land." The entire year, my Provider continually poured His blessings and favor and gifts on me. More than anything He gave me more of Himself. Jesus came closer and I have continually heard the question, "*Do you love me? If I give you the desires of your heart, will you still love Me more?*"

Little did I know that I was being prepared to be a bride for the second time. I would eventually remarry. My Father did give me the desire of my heart. And much more than I bargained for! But this preseason was a critical time of preparation for me. It was a time of deep connection and recommitment to My First Love which was being tested. I found myself daily making the choice to be that sunflower, turning my face toward the Son.

Blessings and success can so easily become seductive and before you know it, the Giver of these gifts can be left in the dust. The greatest danger is that you can be completely unaware that you are drifting away from Him, because of the beautiful distraction that has caught your attention. I found myself being strengthened when I felt weak. Each decision in the moment to walk in obedience was fortifying my core resolve. This was my "sunflower stem" enabling me to turn my face toward the light. I have trained myself to be quick to respond when I am under His conviction. Who we are in secret contains the essence of who we are in reality. And living in the light of the delightful countenance of the Convictor keeps us on a tight leash. I am keenly aware of my human disabilities. I don't know how to love like God yet, but I want to. The fruit from the harvest that was being gathered during this rich and fruitful autumn season was revealing that my motivation to walk in integrity was directly linked to loving my Heavenly Bridegroom well. I no longer wanted to allow my world to be consumed by meaningless activity. I was learning to say "No!" instead of doing things that He was not directing me to do, just because someone was pressuring me.

I am a woman of faith, and I have believed God for impossible things. He has taught me to dream big dreams, God-size dreams and I have no trouble believing in His ability to come through. But then there are days when it is easier to believe that He can perform huge miracles than to believe that I am truly born again. This insecurity comes as the flip-side of a strength that I possess—being a *detail* girl. Sometimes I don't feel like a new creation at all. Just like everyone else, I find myself tripping and stumbling and like the Apostle Paul, *doing the very thing I don't want to do.* On those days, it seems impossible to love God more than I do my own will. That is the moment when I make a decision to turn my face and follow the Son. He knows me, and I am learning to be like the sunflower and lean in by faith to His provision of the newness of life.

Joyful Belief

There are times when life feels like that classroom and I am completely caught off-guard facing a test that I know I am doomed to fail. But maybe that is the point. What better way to confront legalism, which demands perfection in my performance rather than allowing God to show up? Not in a dream but through the life of His Son! For Christ, worshiping His Father meant obeying and extending His hands of mercy towards me. To the beat of His worship, Jesus allowed His hands and feet to be nailed to a cross so that mine might be loosed.

Our life in Christ is not about us pulling an A+ on an exam, knowing all the answers, or being prepared for the unexpected. It is about the power of Love that is graciously released as we humbly walk with our Maker. It is loving a Savior whose mercy has cut through the bindings of our sinful nature and has set us free. And every step we take towards acknowledging our desperate need and believing that all of heaven views us through the Eyes of joyful delight... and believing in ourselves, our new being in Christ, is like another downstroke of the hammer breaking the power of the lies that have held us captive.

Helen Keller said, "Keep your face to the sunshine and you cannot see the shadows. That is what sunflowers do." I love that! It is my deepest desire to embrace this new identity. What a great picture of freedom. Sunflowers are perfectly named and one of my favorite flowers. The stems are tall and sturdy. They are designed by the Great Gardener to bend and twist, enabling the flower to follow the rays of the sun throughout the day. These beauties are known for their strength and hardiness, their productivity and brilliant color. Sunflowers are a symbol of faith, loyalty and adoration.

This was more than a dream. This became a turning point of revealed identity and an invitation to believe, to surrender from striving, and to rest afresh in the assurance of Acceptance. Perfect Love sees me!

Being prepared for this Teacher has never been about being able to regurgitate facts. Being ready means showing up with a hungry heart. Believe. *Be* in agreement with Truth. *Be* one whose eyes are captivated by Glorious Beauty and can't help but worship. This Holy One is so much more than a merciful Teacher! And we are so much more than just His pupils! "*Be*"... "*In*"... such small words, and yet they carry mammoth implications for us as God's children. It was *in* the Heart of God that we were imagined, created and named. His Being is where we come from. It is *in* our decision to return to Him that positions us, to just *be* His child—to rest *in* the security of revealed truth that we *be*long, we have been *in*vited *in,* grafted *in,* adopted *in*to the perfect, loving Family—the GODHEAD! It is *in* Christ where we explore over a lifetime and discover who we really are. We are His offspring, the heirs of Father, Son and Holy Spirit, and it is our standing within this Trinity Family identity which defines us. What a relief that our relationship is never based on our behavior. And never on our performance. It is the mysterious power of Love being channeled through unconditional acceptance that motivates change. And somewhere within the daily grind of the pressures and stressors, you and I are being transformed. As Image-bearers, we choose to remain close to Him and ever so slowly—just like an infant grows to be a toddler, who grows into a child, who transforms into a teenager, who matures into an adult—we will grow *in* His likeness, from glory to glory.

Leaning In:

- What lies have bound and shaped you, like the Bonsai?

- In what areas of your life do you see yourself striving?
- What do you believe would happen if you stopped striving?
- How have you experienced being in God's family?
- What does it feel like to be invited in to just be yourself?

He entered into the very world he created, yet the world was unaware. He came to the very people he created to those who should have recognized him, but they did not receive him. But those who embraced him and took hold of his name were given authority to become the children of God!
(John 1:10-12, TPT)

13

AIRBORNE

DUSTY DISCLOSURE

We were building a house. Not just any house. It's ours. Our dream home! All my adult life, I invested my time and effort working on projects for someone else. I cleaned, painted, stained, wallpapered, and even chinked a log lodge that others owned. At last, a lifetime of longing, a heart's desire was being fulfilled. This time it was ours.

My new husband and I were saving some money by assisting with the staining. We were also helping with the cleanup. There were many log accents in our new home. Each post and beam was going through an intense process of being hand-hued and sanded. Because it was winter, all this finish work was being done inside the shell of the house. Needless to say, the entire building was now thoroughly coated by a thick layer of powdery fir. At the moment it looked more like a sawmill rather than the cozy nest I had envisioned.

My job was to sweep, vacuum and get ready for staining. For the most part, I knew that with every swish of the broom I was creating a massive cloud of dust. The first day I got out the dust mask to protect my lungs. The second sweeping I became a little sloppy and didn't bother with the mask. I wasn't really thinking about the quality of the air until I stepped into the light. Standing still, the rays from the sun-exposed the hidden storm of particles that had engulfed me.

As I walked outside for my next breath of oxygen, I started thinking about perception and, in this case, my lack of self-awareness. I'm the one who stirred the pot. It was MY broom which created the dust bowl. But until stepping into the light, I was oblivious to the magnitude of the consequences of my action. One push of the broom and the whole atmosphere around me became unsettled.

What else am I not seeing as I am rushing through life? What effect is my life having on the world around me? How do I develop a heart that is aware? Do I have the eyes to see and ears to hear? Am I walking in Light or am I blindly forging ahead on my own?

Do you think the Lord would lead us into a testing situation or orchestrate an event in our lives, knowing that we will fail? Outwardly, the thought behind this question seems cruel. Why would a loving Father do that? The Word says that *He does not tempt us.* (James 1:13) But He does test and lovingly discipline His children. If there are areas of pride, arrogance, vanity or anything that would want to steal our hearts away from Him—then YES! Absolutely! The Spirit who convicts will faithfully cover us in mercy and then lead us straight into a situation that will expose our hidden motives and sin. Indeed, the Restorer will orchestrate a sweeping learning experience to reveal the depths of our ignorance and need.

Sometimes I feel like one of those flying insects that swarm to the beacon emanating from the bug zapper that was on my dad's deck. It is truly a fatal attraction! I am so drawn to Jesus, the Light of the world. His kindness is like a holy laser, and the second I hit it, there can be a volt of electrifying revelation. At times the insight ends up frying my fleshly sin, but always there is an invitation to exchange the negative for a positive! It is consistently specific conviction and an extremely clear magnification of the broken places needing healing or sin issues. And then... Love waits for my response. He stands with arms open wide, ready to receive. His heart intent is to remove all that harms and binds me, to heal and give me freedom. But that can only take place with my permission and surrender.

Seed Actions

Jesus is not like the condemner, heaping shame and guilt in an attempt to humiliate and cripple me. One of my worst mistakes was something that I did with the best intentions. I was not being rebellious. I was just young and lacked wisdom. Honesty has always been one of my most treasured values. I had been taught to surround myself with trustworthy individuals who will hold you accountable for your actions. In this case, in a moment of honesty, I shared what was in my heart with the wrong person. He was not trustworthy. And I quickly learned that there are times when you need to hold your tongue and shut your mouth, especially if you don't know the person very well.

Sowing and reaping is the Biblical word picture describing our seed actions which will bring a full harvest of consequences. In this life, we will reap what we have sown. But since my task in this story involves sweeping, I will stay with that image. As the Holy Counselor led me into the light, it exposed my blindness caused by my immaturity. I was absolutely convinced that I was doing the right thing. But as it turned out, I was completely in the wrong. Without realizing it, with one swish of the broom, one motion done in foolish ignorance, a dust storm formed that would take years to settle. I was totally unaware that my broom, my movement, would compromise the purity of air for all of us living in close proximity.

There are some decisions that in the moment seem like no big deal, but from God's perspective, they are serious and can lead to disaster. Tremble in awe and respect His compassionate discipline, because He is a brilliant Father! It is essential to our maturity to lovingly demand that we thoroughly clean up the mess we have made. But even for those whose failure has activated a chain of events creating a catastrophic hurricane force destroying everything in its path, our Savior has you covered. True repentance is always met with forgiveness. The Godhead has already paid the price for the damage and for the necessary restoration. Only They are capable of rebuilding all of the lives involved.

Blind

There are some children who have a rebellious nature that refuse to see the God who has revealed Himself through His creation both around us and in us. Romans 1:19 suggests that it is possible for a person to *push the truth away from themselves* and deliberately choose to believe and live a lie. The most painful season in my life was caused by one of those rebellious ones. I became the target of this person's twisted "truth." The story being told was full of exaggerations and some blatant lies, and when the dust settled, all that was left was broken relationships, grief and tremendous loss.

In all honesty, I think we all have a tendency to run from truth, especially when it comes to owning up to our own mistakes, weaknesses and sin. This self-inflicted blindness is witnessed at its worst within the religious, pious, hardened heart. Jesus taught that pride is a guaranteed blind guide. A prodigal or a Pharisee, the problem is the same. Anything that originates from an elevated sense of self—self-effort, self-protection, self-promotion, self-centeredness, or self-righteousness, anything that we fashion in isolation apart from God creates a contaminated universe without oxygen. The more we play god, thinking that our wisdom is the supreme truth, the deeper we are pulled into our toxic fog of deception.

Sometimes it is not a conscious decision to leave the Light. It is more like drifting. This complacency decides distance rather than dependence. We become focused on other things, sometimes good things and before long we are carried away. We can become completely unaware of the chasm that stretches between us and home until one day we stop and look up. The gracious groan of a Loving Father sends a burst of light across our path that stops us short. For a split second the rays of Mercy unveil the hidden dusty void, and the doorway of grace opens to our world, flooding our hearts with pure fresh air. This was one of those, *Great is his faithfulness; His mercies begin afresh each morning* moments. (Lamentations 3:23, NLT)

Without Jesus, this wood frame was really, in the end, a potential pile of timber. It's the master Carpenter who was truly building His home here and it's in my heart. I am the one who was under construction.

Leaning In:

- How do you see yourself being "under construction?"
- Where have you experienced the light of Jesus shining on your actions which might have caused a "disruption in the atmosphere?"
- What was your heart's response to His conviction?
- What might He be leading you to do to clean up your mess?

Even though the Lord may allow you to go through a season of

hardship and difficulty, he himself will be there with you. He will not hide himself from you, for your eyes will constantly see him as your Teacher. When you turn to the right or turn to the left, you will hear his voice behind you to guide you, saying, 'This is the right path; follow it.'
(*Isaiah* 30:20-21, *TPT*)

14

REFINER'S FIRE

I AM . . . NOT

I find computers to be completely mystifying. With fingers poised on the keypad, I am confident. I am in control. I AM CREATOR! It is a machine. It exists to serve me. I agonize for hours attempting to find just the right words; artistic vessels worthy of holding the fragile treasures being unearthed within the depths of my soul. Then, to my absolute horror, my finger brushes ever so slightly against some unseen key and my masterpiece vanishes. Unsaved and lost forever, swept away. In an instant, an invisible hand hits the delete button and I am left with a blank page. I am caught off-guard. I am speechless. Words dissolve into a groan that actually communicates very clearly what I am feeling. I sit back with my eyes closed and just drift. I have been here before. What just happened? My life was in the flow, in control, amazing—until...

Sometimes circumstances just leave us staring into the blank screen of helplessness, wondering and asking, "What just happened?" The last few years of my life have felt like that.

There is a song that we used to sing on a regular basis at Church. The chorus says, "Refiner's fire, my soul's one desire is to be... holy... Set apart for You, Lord. I choose to be... holy. Set apart for You, my Master. Ready to do Your will." My life prayer has been, "Lord, maximize my life!" I squirm as I write this. What was I thinking, singing that song and praying such a bold prayer? Had I taken some time to explore what it would be like to experience the process of refining... I would have bailed, backed out, run, hid! But it was too late. He had heard me. The One Who hears and answers, the One Who is the Master Jeweler, the Brilliant Refiner of Gold, answered, and He stoked the fire. My choices and circumstances set in motion the most remarkable, cleansing, life-changing experience I have ever lived through; one involving trauma, failure, betrayal and loss—all of which are in the process of revealing My Designer's sanctifying touch on this child who said yes to becoming a new creation in Christ Jesus!

Demolition

For me, this has been a three-fold procedure and revelation. The first involved a methodical dismantling of my self-image which revealed *who I am not*. The second phase exposed what was hidden in the hearts of those around me who were impacted by my refining process and the third is the finale, which promises rebuilding, redeeming, and restoring. This revelation is emerging from the ash and I suspect will follow me into eternity. Who I am is being established, and more importantly, Whose I am is taking the lead in ruling and reigning my inner world!

It all began with a change, actually two HUGE changes. These were not changes in location or profession; these involved first, entering a new season, which Mom always called the "change of life." That would be one of the greatest understatements of all time. I refer to this frightening time as my Menopausal Morph, and it was not a pretty sight. Secondly, I made a choice to remarry —certainly not the greatest decision, not the wisest move to get remarried just as you are embarking on THE greatest melt-down this woman would ever face! But who knew? In 20/20 hindsight I have to admit, it provided the perfect ember storm to position me for the cleansing process. He heard me call Him Master and sing, "Ready to do Your will!"

The Morph

I am naturally a take-charge kind of girl. I love to work hard and thoroughly enjoy a good challenge. I see a problem. I seek solutions, manage others and organize the tasks until the last job gets done. However, upon entering my fifties, something began to shift. I found myself entering this foggy *Twilight Zone* existence. My brain seemed to short-circuit. I couldn't concentrate and I would lose my words. Loud noises would register as pain in my body. Out of the blue, the inside of my gut would burst into an inferno of heat that would sweep over my entire body. The room would begin to close in on me and a feeling of panic would leave me reeling. I remember being in a grocery store one day with my husband when this fiery back-draft hit. I bolted away from him and his friend who were in the middle of a conversation, pushed the cart to the register and in a daze began to unload the food onto the counter as quickly as I could. I was oblivious to the fact that I had cut someone off who was headed for my line. At that moment, beads of sweat were forming on my face, the racket coming from the crowd hit my ears like fingernails scratching across a blackboard and every cell of my body felt like it was going to explode into flames. All I could think of was air. I needed silence and some air!

Needless to say, my daytime "I have it all together" façade, which had always been my go-to elevated refuge providing the illusion of protection and security, was going up in smoke. And then the night terrors hit. Not nightmares, but the terror of knowing that bedtime was approaching and I couldn't sleep. I was constantly tossing and turning, having hot flashes and feeling the added tension of being in a new marriage, attempting to share the bed with a man who had his own sleep issues, which I will not go into. After months of this torturous struggle, I was sleep-deprived, my energy level tanked, and I simply could not function. I stepped out of my management position in the family business and desperately tried to find help. Nothing the doctor offered gave me any relief. There were days that felt like some alien had implanted it's horrible, ugly being inside my body, and I became like a reactive puppet. This being had no tolerance, no patience, and absolutely no nurturing ability.

One of my girlfriends, who was also experiencing her own "morphing" experience, had a husband with a great sense of humor. He gave his wife's alias a pet name—"Hulga." He grew to understand that when Hulga entered the room, he needed to back off and give her irritation plenty of space and tons of grace. I thank God for my women buddies who lived through the heat of this battle with me. They gave me encouragement and laughter which helped immensely to somewhat normalize the craziness we were all experiencing.

One morning I read a verse in Habakkuk that cut me to the core. My eyes focused on the words, ... *they are deeply guilty, for their own strength is their god.* (Habakkuk 1:11, NLT) I had never considered that my strength as a woman and my ability to work hard like a man could actually become an idol in my life. I immediately recognized that this pride was attached to my value system demanding excellence. In my past history, I had the ability to perform well and get beautiful results in whatever I did, but somehow that talent had weaseled its way into the holy realm of my identity and was receiving the attention and worship that belongs only to God. Idolatry is intolerable and destructive and will most assuredly be revealed and destroyed in all of us children who are called by His Name. It was my turn. My idol was exposed and burning and destined for the ash heap.

Day in and day out, I struggled to pull up, but I couldn't. Never in my life had I dealt with physical health issues or depression like this. Some days it was a challenge to get myself out of bed. Not only did I not have the energy to pull off the smallest household tasks, but I especially struggled to have the emotional energy to engage in all of the new relationships that were part of the marriage package. I would discover years later that I also had Lyme Disease, which I suspect was hugely responsible for my decline in health. In the beginning, I forced myself to attend church and family gatherings. But whatever was happening within my being made me feel so awkward and claustrophobic, I just wanted to run and hide.

The Battle Zone

Have you ever had "if only" conversations? "If only I had kept my mouth shut! If only I had just walked away! If only I had not been so blind! If only... if only..." To be human is to be flawed, and at some point in our journey, we will have regrets. I was definitely at that point! My heart was filled with regret and shame. I felt alone, and my downcast eyes condemned me to roam in a dark cavern, dampened by the tears and sweat of my battling soul. The depression would fixate on where I was not measuring up. My weaknesses seemed to be under the magnifying glass, and it felt like I was facing a future without resolve or hope which was driving me into the shadows. I felt like a weary contender, fighting for my sanity. I was ruthless with the weak, sickly stranger staring back at me in the mirror. I loathed myself and became the accuser, jabbing at my weakening self-confidence. My own judgments were ripping away at my self-worth. There was no mercy. (Not helpful!)

Added to this internal battle, I was very aware that I was letting a lot of people down. I could feel the hidden jeers and secret, critical conversations being spoken about me behind my back by family members. Avoidance became my companion and shame, my heavy cloak. I was being crushed beneath the weight of each condemning layer. The depression was determined to strip away all hope of a cure. On the surface, I was trying so hard to be and feel normal. But I was continually exhausted and just couldn't pretend, which led to many conversations with my husband and on-going apologies.

At the time, the emotional pain was so intense, I actually contemplated suicide. That was a wake-up call that drove me in desperation to reach out to a dear friend and mentor, and submit to prayer ministry. To engage God during this lengthy, excruciating trip was exactly the right move. It positioned me to receive His covering and insight and strength to endure. Yes, I whined. I cried. I squirmed. I argued and begged in frustration to feel normal again. Every day during this refining process there was an on-going confession pouring from my repentant heart of who I *was not*—I *was not* God. I *was not* in control. I *was not* perfect or patient or kind. I *was not* productive or a fun wife. The truth is, I didn't really fail every day. Some days were better than others. But overall I felt like a worthless piece of trash! In fact, the condemner and I made a great team, brutalizing my heart for being so weak and unable to buck up like I used to. I was incapable of meeting my own high standards of performance, and I know that I failed to meet the expectations of my husband and his family as well. All I could see at the time was the horror of the dross which filled my "I *am not*" hole and an increasing awareness that I did not fit within this new family.

I hate taking any medication, but I finally gave up and found a drug that gave me a reprieve from the insomnia, and I moved to another bed to sleep. I also got a prescription for an antidepressant that helped me to pull up emotionally. In my holistic approach to healing, I added supplements, took a trip to Idaho and was diagnosed and treated for Lyme Disease, which is now cured.

I didn't understand it at the time, but this magnification of my brokenness would eventually lead to a place of stillness and peace. In the end, my striving nature collapsed, and I allowed my scorched corpse of a soul to be held in the arms of the Comforter. I simply had to decide to embrace my own humanity! Why? Because it is impossible to offer authentic grace and mercy to others without first recognizing your own blatant need. I had to learn to love myself. Grace is the great equalizer. We are all human, bankrupt without it, and desperate to receive mercy, whether we recognize it or not.

The Gold

The refining process always has a purpose. In the context of gold production, it is the final stage that removes impurities and separates the gold from other metals. For us spiritual seekers, Malachi reveals the heavenly purpose—*Listen: I will send my messenger before me to prepare the way. And then the One you are looking for will come suddenly to his Temple—the Messenger of God's promises, to bring you great joy. Yes, he is surely coming, says the Lord Almighty. But who can live when he appears? Who can endure his coming? For he is like a blazing fire refining precious metal, and he can bleach the dirtiest garments! Like a refiner of silver he will sit and closely watch as the dross is burned away. He will purify the Levites, the ministers of God, refining them like gold or silver, so that they will do their work for God with pure hearts.* (Malachi 3:1-3, TLB)

This ordained act of purification is not to destroy us. It really is a brilliant display of loving-kindness which exposes the deeply hidden lies, those which will eventually destroy our priestly nature. Our primary purpose for existence is to love and worship the Almighty. When my identity became compromised by the idol of my own strength and performance, my Refiner's passionate, jealous love came-a-calling. The intensity of Holy fire generated by His Love drove me into the flames of cleansing grace. My surrender to the process transformed the furnace of my circumstances into an encounter that left a unique, divine imprint of His Grace nature branded onto mine.

You and I became the temple under the new covenant of grace. It is His grace that saves us. And it is the same grace He extends to us when we cannot stand to face Him, as the Holy One begins to *"bleach"* our hearts. This merciful gift of Love that sets us free, cost Jesus His life and it will not be compromised by our presumptuous and useless effort to earn it, which is exactly what I was attempting to do.

What I am learning is that faulty identity issues are constructed deep within our hearts and are so easily hidden, both from others and especially from ourselves. We can be absolutely unaware of the reality that our entire being has latched on to what we do, to our position or performance, or what we have accomplished and that leaves us vulnerable. With this unstable foundation, our sense of value and our worth can be gone in one second! My false identity was becoming a tower built on the unstable, shifting sand of my pride, based on my abilities, my successes, and my self-righteousness. In essence, all I was producing was an idolatrous performance, an impotent attempt to fill the deep need I had for acceptance. It was this filth that was consumed in His blaze.

It doesn't matter what we are doing; if it is coming from a motivation to try to earn acceptance and love from God or man, we *are not* depending on Christ alone, His work on the cross, or His ability to be the change agent in our lives. We *are not* moving in faith and our self-effort and pride are blinding us. We are in grave danger of stumbling over the Rock of our salvation. In the words of Romans—*But the Jews who tried so hard to get right with God by keeping the law, never succeeded. Why not? Because they were trying to get right with God by keeping the law and being good instead of by depending on faith.* (Romans 9:31-32, TLB)

Cocoon of Grace

Listen to this scripture in The Passion Translation: *Now, if anyone is enfolded into Christ, he has become an entirely new creation. All that is related to the old order has vanished. Behold, everything is fresh and new.* (2 Corinthians 5:17, TPT) I was experiencing the reality of *being enfolded into Christ... becoming an entirely new creation.* I prayed for this! Without realizing what I was asking, I invited Him to envelop me, to surround me as if with folds or layers of Himself. The nail-scarred hands of my gracious Hero held my soul. His covering and loving-kindness enveloped me, forming a cocoon of hope, the promise of new life. Within that cocoon, I felt like I was going to die! Later I would discover that a holy fear—an intense reverence and awe of the Lord—was being deposited within every cell of my being as I felt His tender hand reshaping me.

I didn't see it then, but I can now. At the very moment I entered the menopausal morphing season, my old striving nature began to fail. The web of depression and condemnation was meant to imprison me. And just like the body of a caterpillar begins to digest itself within its cocoon, my self-loathing judgment and hatred of myself began melting down every fiber of the identity I had constructed from my past performance. I was living out, truly experiencing the favored, paradoxical Kingdom theme—He was replacing the old for the new. On the other side of this refining, He was offering beauty for ashes, the oil of joy for a spirit of fainting. To find my life, I had to lose it. To experience Grace, I needed to see into His eyes. He was manifesting as the Truth, and it was setting me free.

You know what became the most profound realization within my personalized furnace? Even though there were terrifying moments where I felt alone, I was not! Just like the three young Israelites thrown into the fiery furnace, the Son of Man was in it with me. He stood over me watching carefully as the dross was burned away. There was never shame or anger in His eyes, only compassion and longing. Perhaps the same longing that He had as He faced the Samaritan woman at the well. You see, He also has *If only* conversations. *If you only knew who I am and the gift that God wants to give you—you'd ask me for a drink, and I would give to you living water.* (John 4:10, TPT) In my case, the Hands of Grace reached for me within the fire, held my face and said, "*If only you knew who you were created to be. If only you knew that you are Mine, My Beloved. If only you knew that you are fully accepted, fully embraced right here and now in the midst of your sickness and inabilities.*"

He was not judging me. He was judging the lofty false identity that was finding justification and worth based upon performance. He was purifying me—separating ME from falsehood and lies. Every step of the way, I ran to Him. We met in the secret place of my heart, daily wrestling through the pain of failure until finally my will surrendered in exhaustion and I could honestly say, "I give up! You know best. Do what needs to be done."

Before this experience I knew the scriptures about grace, I sang about it, I talked about it. But being stripped down to nothing, being incapacitated and gazing into the eyes of Grace, seeing no condemnation, no accusation, no disapproval, experiencing nothing but pure, loving-kindness and delight when I was at my worst was truly transforming. He wanted nothing from me. He expected nothing. He knew me. He saw me empty and longing to be filled, dying but reaching out for life, and hopeless, yet hanging on every word He spoke.

So, this is Love! This is what it feels like to be pursued, rescued and never abandoned. Truth was being etched onto my heart. This refining work was about knowing Jesus in a deeper way which allowed me to know myself. I experientially felt His kindness when I was unkind. I saw His tenacious loyalty to not leave me in my despair. And most importantly, I witnessed the power of a righteous Judge condemning the lies and deception that were out to destroy my true identity and nature. I truly believe there was no other way for me to see my unhealthy state and for Him to gain permission to access this deep place within my heart. I was desperate for help and truth. When He goes for the gold, radical and excruciating cleansing measures are at work. He is completely dedicated to loving us well, which involves giving us the eyes to see the truth about ourselves which can at times be horrifying.

Perfect Timing

Refining is a timing issue. Now as I write this, my confidence in our relationship is solid, forged over decades of witnessing His unchanging faithfulness, and my Father's on-going discipline has always been a part of that. Running to Him was my default mode for life. Somehow, this heated encounter with the Holy One was very different from receiving discipline. This was more like a sovereign invitation, one that came wrapped in mystery and paradox. His desire was to draw nearer so that I might partake of His Divine Nature. But the moment He draws close, we are exposed first to His radiant purity, followed by a gaze into our own vulnerable mortality. This is where the "fear of the Lord" kicks in! He is the only Righteous One and when His purity and light show up, our impurity is uncovered, lit up, front and center! The only appropriate response is to hit the deck.

His longing for me was the same as mine—to love from a transformed nature that looked like Him. It was critical to experience the power of pure grace, not just be a spectator with head-knowledge; knowing the rhetoric but lacking the experiential impact. Perhaps this is where the truth from Luke comes into play, *She has been forgiven of all her many sins. This is why she has shown me such extravagant love. But those who assume they have very little to be forgiven will love me very little.* (Luke 7:47, TPT) Without this moment of heightened awareness of our miserable state, it is impossible to appreciate the depth of the precious gift of mercy and forgiveness being offered to us. (I am not suggesting that we stay here. It is just a humbling reference point!) This was my moment to see, to feel, and to know how absolutely gentle, understanding and gracious my Heavenly Father really is at an entirely new level.

Hidden Judgment

Eventually, my energy began to return and life became more manageable. Never had I experienced grace and mercy like this! Those dark years reinforced the ongoing work in my life—to be more gentle and compassionate with myself. Looking back, probably the most important thing being revealed during this blaze was the contrast between the true and only Righteous judgments of God and the critical judgment that I had towards myself, as well as the judgment that I was receiving from outsiders. This unrighteous human judgment is what ushered in the second wave of refining.

There is a reason we are commanded to *Judge not!* The Passion Translation puts it this way: *Refuse to be a critic full of bias toward others, and judgment will not be passed on you. For you'll be judged by the same standard that you've used to judge others. The measurement you use on them will be used on you. Why would you focus on the flaw in someone else's life and yet fail to notice the glaring flaws of your own?* (Matthew 7:1-3) My tailor-made furnace-revelation exposed my own unrighteous judgment executed by myself and others in my inner circle.

I love the way the Holy Spirit revealed this.

I was babysitting my grandson, Eli, who was about twenty months at the time. He grabbed my shoes from the basket and ran and dropped them at my feet. Then holding my hand, he awkwardly placed each tiny foot into the enormous opening of my size six Adidas and began his labored walk across the room. As I watched him, a knot formed in my gut. He was adorable. However, what I began to realize about myself was not so cute.

This was a perfect portrayal of our human, striving effort to be God. We place ourselves in the Creator's shoes, climb upon His throne and play Judge. As if we could ever have the inside story about another person's heart! Our opinions take on a life of their own, staging an imaginary world, one that is scripted and ordered by the little, "i am." As if our take on any matter is ever completely accurate! We make our plans and set the course. As if we have the wisdom and knowledge and foresight to walk this path alone! We are all guilty. There is no righteous one. For me, I took the opportunity within this fire to own up. I was guilty of judging both myself and others. And I experienced the reality of *the measurement you use on them will be used on you.*

Confession is the doorway to receiving the forgiveness and release that we all need. I found an immediate response from Jesus. Grace offered His faithful hand, aiding my descent from the lofty precipice where pride had led me. The atmosphere of self-elevation leaves all of us dizzy and disoriented and completely dependent on God's Spirit to safely guide us home. In reality, what I discovered was that I am much more secure as an adult person when I just admit that I am a child who belongs in the arms of the perfect loving Judge Who does know the inside scoop on

EVERYTHING. I am loved by God, accepted and valued by Christ, and paradoxically complete in my incompleteness. I am a finished work in process because He has had the last word: *It is finished!*

My Final Note

Over the years, even though my health improved, problems within our extremely dysfunctional and complicated marriage and "blended" family did not resolve. My husband was battling Parkinson and I was carrying most of the load of household responsibilities. Attempting to blend our cultural differences was an ongoing challenge. Our relational root system was too shallow to overcome all the obstacles. The truth is my refining fire revealed more than just what was in my heart. What was hidden came to the surface in the hearts of all. Misunderstandings became judgments, exaggerations and blatant lies were spread about me, trust was shattered, and the marriage could not survive. In the end, my husband's children had an intervention with him with the intent to have him separate from me. Simply put, it is impossible to build a marriage and family when members of the household think the worst about you! Relationships cannot exist in an atmosphere of suspicion and deceit. All connection erodes. I left my home, my marriage failed, my reputation within the community was compromised and the Refiner's Fire has finally come to an end.

My intent in sharing my story is to help, not just those who are in the midst of their own metamorphosis which can only be accomplished through a baptism of fire, but also those who are in the inner circle of the dear one who is engulfed in flames. Everyone needs hope and reassurance that it won't last forever. A woman who is in hard labor needs a birthing partner. Hopefully, she has a supportive, calming loved one who understands the process and can give her the encouragement she needs to endure the pain until the birth is finally over. This is exactly what I needed in the midst of my Refiner's Fire. Those who knew me well fulfilled that critical role for me, and I will be forever grateful! It was tragic and so unnecessary that my story ended the way it did. When it is all said and done, we have no control over others and their actions. We are only responsible for our own lives. I have no idea how everyone else will deal with their failure. I only know that mine is teaching me the importance of extending mercy.

I truly believe that God is on a mission to teach us to believe in others the way He does, allowing us to see each person through His faith-eyes. It is true that each person carries His unique spiritual imprint. It is Tailor-made, a one-of-a-kind stamped expression of the Divine. It is within this belief paradigm that we need to approach each other. To live and move within this God-dream—to BE Image Bearers, His values must become ours. This is especially true when a loved one is being immersed in His Fire. It is Holy ground and both the process, and the person need to be honored. It is a spiritual rebirth at a deeper level. Just as being baptized in water is a Holy moment, so is this. They both bring new life.

I am walking away from this refining experience with a life message: You and I are not defined by the dross. Our names are written in the Lamb's Book of Life, not with the ink from a pen. Our names are etched in blood, embedded for all eternity, onto the pages of His living story. We discover our true and authentic being as we follow His lead—surrendering, laying it all down. Our names are spoken as one—Beloved of God, Bride of Christ, His Temple—the Resting Place of His Love!

Here is what I am discovering about the flip-side to the ultimate agenda of the Refiner's Fire—*all things hidden will come to the surface.* What is left after the dross is burned away is His purified treasure. He has always known who I am, and He is reshaping my identity. I still feel very fragile, but I am leaning into His acceptance. I am quicker now to catch the old familiar lies that criticize my frailty. I am practicing taking those captive and choosing to be in agreement with His word spoken about me. I was only too familiar with who I was not. For the rest of my life and into eternity, I am invited into a new story, as a new character, with a new nature and so are you! We get to explore this territory with Him in total freedom, loved completely by Him.

This was His gift. I will emerge with wings that will lift me into a new realm of faith vision. I am learning that only to the extent that I am able to peer through the shroud of mystery and be immersed and at rest within the paradoxical ways of God, will I be rightly positioned to embrace myself and others. This realm where everything is fresh and new is available the moment we run into the embracing arms of Jesus. But it is within the refining process of "tearing down the old order", where we receive the transforming touch of Grace on our lives to arise as Image-bearers, fulfilling the dream of our Father.

Leaning In:

- What did you learn about God within your refining process?
- What was revealed about you in the fire?
- What God DNA is being branded into your nature through this fire?
- Who has the Lord placed in your life as a "melt-down" partner?
- What is the life message that you have received as a result of walking through your fire?

For in a visitation of the night you inspected my heart and refined my soul in fire until nothing vile was found in me.
(Psalms 17:3, TPT)

A NOTE TO THE READER

WARM REFLECTIONS ON A CHILLY DAY

There is a tree outside my living room window that is laden with snow. Its branches have a natural tendency to droop which seems like an unlikely resting place for the fluffy frock. The wet snow shoulders this evergreen like a saturated oversized white fur. Each bough bends beneath the weight of it until finally, it can bear no more. I am not sure how it happens. Maybe a slight breeze moves the branch ever so lightly, causing the sudden release of its burden. Maybe there is a rebellious snowflake that is sick of sticking around and restlessly causes an avalanche, taking as many fallen flakes with him as he can. Or perhaps the strength of this evergreen is being tested and at long last, the gavel of gravity falls with a crash, bringing some mysterious trial to an end.

There is something about the way this tree was created that enables it to carry the heavy burden of wet snow. If this fir could feel, would it be bogged down with the life that it was destined to live? Would it complain that it was doing all the work? Would it be embittered that it was made with dropping limbs? Would it weep and feel overwhelmed by the load that it was carrying? I wonder.

It actually stands out amongst the rest of the trees. I am

amazed that it doesn't break under the stress. It has captivated my attention. Does it realize how majestic it appears, adorned by the pure white flocking? I wonder if it is relaxed and at peace being a droopy fir tree. What song is being sung beneath the strain of its daily winter tasks? Or perhaps, it doesn't view its purpose as a strain at all but as some kind of parental privilege. The bent limbs seem to cradle and rock the bundle it carries like a contented mother embracing her child.

I am filled with hope as I look at this tree. Hidden within its obvious majestic frame, I catch a glimpse of Compassion, whose very nature bends towards me.

Years ago, with outstretched arms, Jesus caught my fallen sinful heart and carried it to the grave. I fix my gaze on the pure white snow, and I can hear His gentle whisper reminding me again and again of the reality of resurrection. I am forgiven and cleansed. I am a new creation. And there was within this wondrous deed a call, a provision and an assurance that I can be like Him.

The call comes from the deep. It is what entices me to stop, to look, to seek, to listen. There is a Voice that I crave to hear. He is the Word. And it is restful days like today that I soak in God's greatest provision—Presence! The call IS the provision. The call beckons me to come—to BE—IN Christ. It is here, in this position, that I discover my great need. There is no shame here—this confession that I am not enough, that I am lacking. Nothing about me catches Him off guard. On my worst day, when I make mistakes, even in my most agonizing failures, I am invited into gentle correction. Wisdom speaks, and I am embraced with encouragement. There is never condemnation, only acceptance.

This dance within our relationship appears to be the key that unlocks the fullness of life and love. I find it all. I don't have to be afraid of lack. Everything I need lies within me. His mind connects with my mind. His thoughts flow into my thoughts. His emotion moves my emotion. All of Him is available and daily calls to me desiring connection and adoration. He is safe. He is kind. And I am held, just like the glorious bundle that is now glistening in the sunshine outside my window.

May you, dear reader, stand out, stand strong and be deeply rooted in the stillness of your Dream Maker's provision for you. May you discover for yourself how absolutely accepted and loved you are. May you taste and see the expansive Goodness that dwells in the Heart of God towards you as your Creator, your Savior, and your Sustainer. This Goodness holds us and defines us. May you embrace the Truth, as you learn to carry His love for yourself and others. May you weather each season in your life masterfully, whether you feel like the tree laden with snow or one that is burned in the Refiner's Fire.

Thank you for taking the time to journey with me. My hope and prayer is that you were encouraged to lean in, to think deeply about your own life and challenged to reduce the clutter and clammer within your own personal space. Listen for the Whisper. The Voice of Compassion invites you in. You are encouraged to ask and keep on asking, to seek and keep on seeking and knock and keep on knocking. He awaits with the Gift of His Presence. He knocks at your door. He seeks your company within solitude. And He asks that you listen to the infinite ways that He speaks. Listen as He whispers...

Blessed are those who trust in the Lord and have made the Lord their hope and confidence. They are like trees planted along a riverbank, with roots that reach deep into the water. Such trees are not bothered by the heat or worried by long months of drought. Their leaves stay green, and they never stop producing fruit.
(Jeremiah 17:7-8, NLT)

ACKNOWLEDGMENTS

First and foremost, I am so grateful for the inspiration and the faithful, loving touch of the Author of my life and Finisher of my faith. There are some achievements that simply cannot be done without the loving support of dear friends and family, those who are truly an extension and manifestation of my loving Heavenly Father.

To my children, Jamie and Jason—thank you for keeping your eyes on the Only Perfect One, for staying true to who God made you to be, despite the failings of your earthly parents. You are living proof that love endures, faith is resilient, hope is truly an anchor and we can endure every circumstance.

To my best friend, Paula Sue—Your friendship is a priceless gift. What would I have done without you? You have shown me what honor and respect look like. Your encouragement has always been my flickering flame showing up on my darkest days. This book would not exist had it not been for your belief in me. Your words carry birthing power!

To my new friends at Above the Sun, Jesse and Elisheba—When I made the decision to walk off my map into the unknown world of publishing, the Lord led me to you. Thank you for making this such a relaxed and enjoyable ride! I appreciate your creative instincts and your ability to gently guide me through the editing process. I will forever be grateful for your hearts which created an atmosphere of safety and encouragement. It was the perfect environment needed to complete this project.

I also want to acknowledge the great impact that Bethel Coaching has had on the completion of this book. Going through the certification process has been life-changing! Before going through this training, writing a book was just a dream. Coaching turned the dream into a doable goal.

To David Smith—sitting under your teaching has given me a fresh vision for Kingdom discipleship. My heart as a coach is being reshaped as I develop a radical belief in others. Thank you for your faithful investment in our lives.

To Tony Stoltzfus—Your books have changed the course of my life and my paradigm of ministry. I am discovering the brilliance of the coach approach in helping others grow, but that is nothing compared to what is happening in my own heart. I especially appreciate your insight in discovering our "being call, our doing call and our life message." So many "AHA!" moments. Thank you!